SUCCESSFUL AS F*CK

SUCCESSFUL AS F*CK

A No BS Tale of Screwing Up and Succeeding Anyway

Riah Gonzalez

NEW DEGREE PRESS

COPYRIGHT © 2022 RIAH GONZALEZ

All rights reserved.

SUCCESSFUL AS F*CK

A No BS Tale of Screwing Up and Succeeding Anyway

ISBN

979-8-88504-593-3 *Paperback*

979-8-88504-939-9 *Kindle Ebook*

979-8-88504-827-9 *Digital Ebook*

For my senior prom date, whose impressive 'stache fooled everyone into thinking I brought a thirty-year-old to the dance, I love you. Thank you for believing this book will make us a million dollars, believing my words will change lives, and always being down for a crazy idea. You never let me give up on dreaming bigger and reaching farther. Your love makes me a better person.

Our story isn't fully documented in this book, but I lovingly tucked you in these pages, and more importantly, I forever tucked you in my heart. High fives to the eighteen-year-old me who knew you were the one. You saved me a million times, and I don't tell you enough how much I love you for that.

I may have been super late to our wedding, but I won't be late to tell you are stronger than anyone I know. Yours is the real story that needs documenting, yet you sit back and let me shine. Cheers to holding hands until the finish line of life, Amor.

For Angie, my brown-eyed angel. My life began in earnest when I first held you in my arms. We have been to hell and back, and I cannot think of a better person to hold hands with through the fire. Your life is a testament that all things are possible, and I am so fucking proud of you. Never forget any action is good action. Look at all the beauty you create in the world and the people you heal with your special gifts. If you ever doubt how miraculous you are, pick up the phone and call me. I will remind you of how you transformed my life. I will never give up on you—pinky promise.

* * *

For my manifesting miracle, Marisol. Watching you live out your dreams makes me want to stretch out my arms and invite more goodness into my life. You are doing it. I watch you make a new reality for yourself over and over again. Thank you for letting me in and letting me be a witness to the transformation that is possible. Thank you for second, third, and infinite chances. I love your beautiful and kind soul. You were never an afterthought, Pumpkin. My love for you is intentional, and I'll forever work to be the mom you deserve. I love you with my whole heart.

* * *

For Gabriela Maria Grace, the tiny woman who brings us all together. Your hugs are healing hugs. Your laugh can light up an entire room, and it's impossible to feel sad when you are happy. Thank you for being my companion and believing in me when I don't believe in myself. When you tell me I am a good mom, I believe you. Don't forget to always paint them green. There will come a day you'll venture out on your own, but I will treasure this time my whole life. Let's always watch movies we love and make fun of the main characters (Tris. Four. Eyes darting side-to-side). Let's have serious talks and ridiculous chats, and let's always laugh until we almost wet ourselves. You make my life fun.

Contents

INTRODUCTION   11

CHAPTER 1   LIVIN' LA VIDA BROKA   15
CHAPTER 2   THEY LOVE ME, THEY LOVE ME NOT   19
CHAPTER 3   THE OLD FAMILY RECIPE   25
CHAPTER 4   SMOKEY SMOKEY, DIET COKE-Y   35
CHAPTER 5   THE GIRL IN THE CAR   43
CHAPTER 6   THE TASSEL WAS WORTH THE HASSLE   55
CHAPTER 7   BLEND OR ASCEND   67
CHAPTER 8   THE BITTER GRIND   73
CHAPTER 9   A DROP TOO MUCH   81
CHAPTER 10   CRASH INTO ME   93
CHAPTER 11   IN THE MIDDLE   103
CHAPTER 12   THE ANATOMY OF TENACITY   113
CHAPTER 13   ALL HAIL THE SHITTY ROUGH DRAFT   123
CHAPTER 14   BOOM.   131

ACKNOWLEDGMENTS   137

Introduction

It's four o'clock in the morning. There's a crying baby on my lap and a microwave beeping every thirty seconds in the kitchen across the hall letting me know the formula is warm. It won't stay warm if I don't get off my ass. My eyes blur after staring at the same sentence in the same textbook for an hour. If I close my eyes, the words might appear on the back of my eyelids; like the dumb tattoo you get at eighteen and regret forever.

I don't know why I thought I could do this. My daughter continues to fuss. Taking one college course at a time while raising kids and trying to pay the bills is a task "The Woman Who Has It All" does with a smile on her perfectly made-up face. *Maybe I'm not her, after all.* I begin to descend into full-on impostor syndrome panic before I look at my sweet, *loud* child and stop myself.

How can I be sure I'm unsuccessful when I don't know what real *success* even looks like beyond my power-suit fantasy?

"Success is a journey." Barf. We've all seen a version of this sentiment on a hundred motivational greeting cards and embroidered throw pillows, but none of them take it further. What the hell *is* success, anyway? Who decides? Why does every so-called *success story* plaster over the real stuff—the crying on the floor, the talking to God (the Universe, The Higher Power, what-have-you), the exhausted mornings in the car, the Zoom meeting sweatpants—in favor of the same tired platitudes? I want to see a more real version of success in the world.

I'm a normal person with a challenging story. I have made horrible mistakes. I've hurt other people, and I have also shown up the best I could for others. I am beautifully imperfect. I wanted to write a book where I am brave enough to put my shit on blast so others can empower themselves to do the same. It wasn't easy, though. It's easy for me to be vulnerable, but at first, I worried that *fully* telling my truth would make me unlovable to others. Ultimately, I decided the process of writing this book was for me and prayed I could at least be honest with myself. Along the way, I let it all out by clacking away on my keyboard and started the process of healing.

What if you could do the same—get it all out in a way that felt good for you? How would it feel to reveal the 100 percent unfiltered you? Liberating? Scary? Maybe a little of both? Even if you're not ready to open Pandora's box, I believe my story is not unlike many others. I'm a regular person, just with a bigger mouth than most.

Success has more to do with all those little moments that don't make it onto the inspirational poster or syrupy commercial. I believe it takes different forms at different phases of our lives. It can hang out in the shit show of one's early years, busting out into the real world and the equally messy young adulthood. It can grow with you through the seemingly inconsequential struggles and successes after. While it seems counterintuitive, success can hold your hand gently when you hit rock bottom. Yes, even at the bottom, there can be moments where you can win.

Society often says only material things define success: travel around the globe, take vacations whenever, or own a house by the beach (or the home in the heart of the city.) Throughout this book, we will take a journey down a different path. We will explore how you can rock the hell out of your life with no need for cheesy vision boards using magazine clippings. Or, if you do want to keep the vision board, we'll tack up the hard parts too. Acknowledge the struggles, not because we want more tough stuff, but because we often learn the richest lessons there. Reaching your goals and lifting yourself to the next level requires recognizing the places where victory existed all along, but you didn't see it at the time.

There is nothing wrong with aiming for those goals, but don't discount the fact you already have all you need to have unconventional success in life. We will dig into the nitty-gritty of my own journey and who were the positive influences along the way. The strongest contenders for my inspiration were my grandma and three of the most beautiful girls in the world, my daughters. You, too, can learn how to achieve success even from two ladies in their twenties and a twelve-year-old. This book is an exploration of unconventional success and tenacity. They tend to pop up in the most interesting of places.

Maybe you picked up this book because it has the word *fuck* on the cover. That's cool. I make a lot of my decisions that way, too. Maybe you got tired of the pervasive bullshit on social media telling you the only thing standing between you and a Ferrari is working an eighty-hour week. Maybe you want to feel seen in your stumbles in life. No matter why you're here, I'm here with you, ready to spill my guts so you can learn to better listen to yours. Who wouldn't want a juicy window into someone else's clusterfuck-with-a-happy-ending?

I'm here to stand for those of us who've crawled out of difficult places and landed on our feet. Just like our lives are lived in echoes of past, present, and future, this expedition won't be a boring chronological dictation of all my nitties and gritties. It will take you along my journey to success as my brain and heart see it. I'm hopeful your brain and your heart will recognize that adventure too.

This book is for you. You—currently doing your best and hoping it is enough. You, determining what *enough* even means. You, who prays and wonders half the time if anyone is listening. This is for the brave ones who attempt to make sense of all the nonsense of life, love, family, faith, business, and everything in between. You are daring to ask the questions, even if the answers all result in "I don't fucking know."

Are you still with me? Then take a seat and buckle up, bitches. You're in for an interesting ride.

CHAPTER 1

Livin' La Vida Broka

Everyone measures success differently. Many people think money is the only indicator. For others, their education says, "Hey! I made it!" My definition of success continues to evolve through the years. In my early adulthood, I became a wife and a mother. I thought motherhood was the supposed pinnacle of a woman's life. I reached it at only twenty years old. Still, success felt miles away.

The year my first daughter was born, I worked at a discount clothing store part-time. The hours were flexible with my husband's work schedule, and we could not afford childcare. There were a lot of things we couldn't afford. We struggled to maintain our necessities. We lived in a rinky-dink one-bedroom apartment with carpet covering the floor in the kitchen. The only bathroom in the apartment conveniently located inside our bedroom had inexplicable carpeting too. This creative floor plan meant our laundry or messy bed was on full display when we had visitors who needed to use the restroom. Nothing says "welcome to my abode" like a bombed master bedroom. It wasn't a dream situation, but it was ours, and it was home. We made room in our snug bedroom to create a nursery on the wall between the bathroom and the closet. The "nursery" consisted solely of Baby Angie's white crib. We were gifted her Baby Looney Tunes bedding from a local mothers' group, and I loved it.

Work sucked. My brain cells were rotting in the monotony, but we needed to scrape together any pennies we could. It was pennies indeed. I made $6.75 per hour. I asked for more money, but my manager told me that I should be grateful for the "extra pay" they offered. My paychecks were sad, and the work was soul-killing, but I was willing to do whatever was needed if it meant I could provide for my daughter.

My husband worked two jobs and one was at a restaurant. He wasn't the biggest fan of working there, but at least we knew he would get dinner on or after his shifts. During the day, he built his budding career at the shipyards where my dad worked. He tried to hide at lunchtime, but his coworkers often cajoled him into the cafeteria to hang out. We didn't have food at home for him to pack, and there were zero dollars to buy him hot lunch. My dad ended up paying for his lunch daily for two years. I hated accepting his help. It burned, but it was still better than the alternative. (Side note—thank you, Daddy. I have never forgotten your generosity.)

At home, I made do with food bank randomness and WIC (Women/Infant/Children Grocery Program) checks, which only provided some formula, cheese, and milk. Even though we didn't have money for food, the government's threshold for poverty somehow deemed us *well off* enough to fend for ourselves. We didn't qualify for food stamps or other assistance other than WIC. Lunch for me was often a few dry corn tortillas, ripped up and lightly fried with one egg and soggy tomato leftovers. Yummy. I kept dollar store salt and pepper on hand, and it made most meals palatable, regardless of the ingredients.

Anything above survival was irrelevant to daily life. We barely paid the bills, but we made it work. With that covered, we focused all our energy on the one thing truly important—Angelica.

I would ask my husband, "Hey babe, do we have diapers?" He would count them out one by one, "Enough for the next few days." Sweet. Payday was the next day. "How are we on formula?"

I stood in the kitchen and shook the almost empty can. Although I was grateful for the help we received with the formula, it wasn't enough.

"Um... we should make it through until payday. Then we have to figure something out." Maybe I would try to pick up an extra shift to ensure we met her needs.

On the rare occasions Angie would actually nap atop Baby Bugs Bunny or Baby Tweety (because seriously, that kid was an insomniac), I would look down at her mop of dark hair and her cherub cheeks framed by her out-of-this-world eyelashes. Although our financial reality was bleak, this beautiful little girl was evidence that the world couldn't possibly be as cruel as I previously believed. I was valuable, even if the only good thing I would accomplish in my life was being her mom.

Humble beginnings can be a huge wake-up call. There is an abrupt element of loss of innocence when we emerge into the reality of young adulthood. Without previous preparation, you are quickly redefining what a win looks like. Limited resources push many people to find alternative solutions. It's not all bad. Coming into adulthood can be a time of great creativity and ingenuity. Still, challenges present themselves in different ways, and we often wonder how to win the race if we can't reach the finish line.

Here's an option—move the damn line closer. Redefine where the line is, and then celebrate the fuck out of yourself when you accomplish something you previously thought impossible.

I measured success in this snippet of my life in how loved and nourished my child was. It leaned on my ability to keep her clean and wearing the right size clothing. It meant when she cried, I had the tools to care for her: a warm bottle, a fresh diaper, a basic crib to sleep in, and my arms for when the only thing she needed was her mom.

I look back at those moments—the ones where I would stand in the dark apartment bedroom swaying in front of her crib with her in my arms. In many ways, we were not so different, my daughter and I. Barely twenty years old, I was a child myself. We would make it, I decided. In my own small ways, this poor-as-hell momma was succeeding. Safety and love can be our greatest achievements. I looked down at my tiny kiddo—lightly snoring and still sniffling from the tantrum it took to get her to fall asleep—and knew this was only the beginning for us.

This was version 1.0 of our success story. Did I eat at least something that day? Success! Was there at least a dribble of gas in my car? Success! Did I make it another day without the aforementioned car breaking down? Double success!

I was living an adult life with a teenager's brain. It wasn't an ideal start, but I wouldn't change it. I appreciate simpler things now because of the beginning I had. I reached higher because I was an example for my daughter and her sisters who would follow. Everyone starts somewhere, and this was my foundation for a lifetime of growth and of remeasuring my accomplishments along the way.

CHAPTER 2

They Love Me, They Love Me Not

A limiting belief tells us that being alone means our life will be unseen, and our accomplishments will be empty. We imagine scenarios where the heartache breaks us.

I once imagined achieving a master's degree, then walking out on stage during the commencement. I looked up to the stands and saw that no one was there clapping and whistling for me. Only strangers. I *needed* someone there. I needed someone in the crowd to lock eyes with who sent me the mental message, *I saw what you did to get here. I'm so fucking proud of you.*

Bridging the gap between alone and not alone can be scary. Intimacy requires the highest level of authenticity and vulnerability. Are you ready to go there with someone? Are you ready to show all sides of yourself, including letting someone see what you have been hiding from yourself?

Rejection sucks balls. It hurts and brings up a shit-ton of insecurity. Although our whole being tells us the contrary, being rejected doesn't mean we are not worthy. It's possible the needs of the person rejecting us were simply elsewhere. I'm not minimizing the visceral response that being passed over or overtly turned away brings to the surface. It's real. It burns because rejection is not only the distress of being pushed away. It's often the fear of not having a witness to our lives. This false assumption tells us without the approval or presence of another, we are not whole.

Maybe you suffer in silence when there are people who love you, but you can't let them in. They care about you—your partner, your badass friends who call daily, or a tight-knit family you wish would be a little less uptight and up in your biz. Your dread of being rejected isolates you in a way where even the ones who love you can't get in. This dread tucks you gently into a safe box of what is comfortable and what you deem acceptable. Without venturing from the comfort zone, how can they cheer for you?

My first memories of rejection still make me sad. I was in third grade, and there was a boy named Gabe Walker. He had light brown hair, blue eyes, and a smile that could melt any nine-year-old's heart. I decided he was the love of my life. We were going to get married and buy a house with a white picket fence. I imagined our future happiness. In real life, Gabe and I were just friends and would hang out at recess. I didn't make friends easily, which made our relationship extra special.

One day, a gaggle of girls (miraculously including me) formed a caucus to determine who would be Gabe's next girlfriend. We deliberated for the entirety of recess over who deserved the title but couldn't come up with a solution.

Then Gabe sauntered over to our circle because he saw multiple friends in it, "Hey, guys. What are you doing?"

The leader of the pack stood with her hands on her hips and declared, "We're deciding who you are going to go out with next."

Gabe looked surprised. "Uh, er, oh, okay."

There was no longer much to discuss since the subject of the conversation accidentally crashed the party. Gabe and I walked back to the classroom together, our steps in a synced cadence. He stopped, turned to me, and said, "I haven't decided. It's between you and Whitney Johnson."

My heart fluttered. I could not believe I was in the top two!

"You're so nice, and you're a good friend, but she's so pretty... I don't know how to choose between you."

I stopped walking, in shock.

I wanted to stab his eyes out. *Why can't I be the pretty one?* I mean, *YAY*, he thinks I'm nice! But why can't I be nice *and* pretty?

Ultimately, he did choose me, and for two glorious hours, I was the girlfriend of Gabe Walker... until the next recess when someone made fun of him for going out with me, and he dumped me unceremoniously. My little world came to a crashing end. My sweet dream of love disappeared in one dramatic instant.

Rejection doesn't mean complete and utter dismissal forever. While the story of Gabe and I ended on the blacktop after our one-day relationship, the story of the love of my life didn't. Life went on. I made new friends and dated other people eventually. Again, I found rejection from people who decided I wasn't as pretty or said I was nice but not nice enough. Time passed and each rejection eventually led me to my husband. He doesn't compare me to anyone else. He accepts all of me. The way I now accept all of myself.

I've committed to bringing my true self into my deeper relationships in the last several years. There are two sides to Riah Gonzalez: the public, professional, and getting-to-know-you side and the sensitive, tender, inner circle side. Previously,

I wore a mask for my acquaintances because I wanted them to feel comfortable. The *real me* could be too much, too raw, or too emotional.

Can we make a pact? Let's lean into who we really are. It can be a challenge because society teaches us from an early age how we should behave—polite and bland; soft-spoken with no real opinion or voice worth hearing because *too much* often means *not enough*.

But I'm here to tell you I am definitely too much, and that's not a bad thing. Maybe you are too much. We can all be too much and *still be more than enough*, and it is time for us to start showing it.

Success resists the internal desire to dim your soul's light. It's natural to fear letting out our authentic selves. Overcoming that fear and succeeding is equal to gripping the knob on the lamp of your soul and cranking it all the way up to the brightest setting it will go. You will know you are smack dab in the middle of success when there's no hiding for fear, you'll blind someone with the light of your greatness. You can be unapologetically you, and you'll likely wonder what took you so long. Scary and exhilarating? Yes, but oh so worth it.

You are a divine being deserving of the love and appreciation of being seen. You hold the light of your true self, so why in the fuck would you hide in the shadows?

Rejection isn't something worth avoiding. Be affected by its sting but don't allow it to choke your progress. Shying away from our birthright of self-acceptance will only make us more stagnant than before. The hard work of achieving success may not seem worth getting up for—until finally, one day, it all clicks: "This is me!" We can embrace who we really are without worrying what others think because rejection never truly controlled us anyway! We possessed the power all along. In the end, it's not how much money you make or what your job description is. It's going to come down to whether you reached in and grabbed ahold of life with both hands or stood frozen in fear.

If you need to cry, let it pour out. Don't lock away your pain and emotions. Let them wash over you until you've found comfort from the love of the person you need the most: yourself. We are much more than what the world tells us and what we tell ourselves. We are our voices, our emotions, and our passions. Throw away your masks and proudly be okay with your shit show of gloriousness.

This is us. This is me. I'm tired of apologizing for who I authentically am, and you should be tired too. It's time to accept ourselves and say "fuck you" to anyone who judges us because we're too loud, too opinionated, or too passionate. If you feel broken, let yourself be broken for a while. Sometimes we need to break in order to put ourselves back together even stronger.

CHAPTER 3

The Old Family Recipe

I'd like to say I'm classy sassy, but I'm probably more of a pain in the (s)ass. I have often wondered where in the world I get my *wit* from. After some soul searching, I finally figured out who influences my internal dialogue and sassy tone. The answer came as such a relief. It was not a random voice. It was someone very familiar.

If I didn't know my dad was adopted, I could have sworn I was the shiny apple that biologically fell from my paternal grandmother's lovely, complicated tree. We both cussed more than a little, valued achieving big things, and kept loving others the best we could despite frequently messing it up. I learned to truly embrace my authentic self by looking up to Grandma Carol.

Carol Dore Billington was a firecracker. She spoke her mind, even if it hurt your feelings. Radical candor that stung didn't conflict with her devout spirituality though. She attended St. Thomas Episcopalian Church religiously (hah!) each Sunday at the early service.

When I attended with her and my grandpa, it was my job to sit next to her and wake her up if she slumped over asleep. Darn narcolepsy was serious to her, but to a child it was hilarious. Here's this short, commanding woman who accidentally falls asleep in the wooden pew. I would look over at her when she'd begin to snore gently for the third time. *Poke.* Why even bother going to church if you aren't even awake for the service? But hey, it gave me something to do during the exhausting process of standing up and sitting down over and over again. The monotone hymns only enhanced this boredom.

The congregation sang, "Holy, holy, holy! Lord God Almighty!"

I mouthed the words, *Why am I the o-o-o-only one who wants to leeeaaavvve?* Meanwhile, Grams stirred long enough to pass me the hymnal with a pointed look. I lifted my voice audibly in song. *Oops. Busted.*

After church, it was off to the Red Lion for the Sunday breakfast buffet. We always invited friends. Sometimes the priest came along, sometimes the organ player—there was a rotating cast of the Billington Buddies Brunch Bunch (pending trademark). I usually tuned out most of the conversation, honing in instead on the massive amounts of food.

"I see you over there, young lady," Grandma Carol said across the table. "Don't be greedy and don't be wasteful." We both knew what she was really saying. *You're fat, and you don't need to get any fatter.*

I learned early on that your biggest inspiration can also cut you to the core. Her love could have edges and zero filters. She told me when I was twelve, "You get fatter and fatter every time I see you." I hid with the upstairs rotary phone and secretly called my dad collect. I sobbed and told him what Grandma said.

Although we lived forty-five minutes away, my dad grabbed the keys and rushed over to speak with Grandma in person. I tucked myself away in the upstairs guest room when he arrived on the scene. I heard the front door open, and when the heated conversation began, I crawled on my apparently offensive belly to the top of the stairs to listen in.

"Mom, you *can't* say things like that to her! She's twelve. Also, you know she's sensitive."

"Well, Jimmy, I say it the way I see it. I have struggled with my weight my whole life, and I worry about her. I'm trying to help."

Her "help" still rings in my head, the echo of insults past. It distinctly did *not* help. This would not be the first or the last time someone would "help" with their comments about my body size.

She did other weird things too, like leaving the price tag on all our gifts and pointing it out each time. "Girls, I spent a lot of money on these gifts. You need to take care of them." Apparently, we were savages who needed reminders on how to perform basic care of presents. I never quite knew how to respond.

She bought the same thing for my dad on all his birthdays and every Christmas: white socks, tighty-whities, and tank top undershirts. He would squeeze the packages and look over at my sisters and me. "I wonder what this could be? I have no idea! Girls, can you guess what it might be?"

"Well, Jimmy, I just don't want you getting into an accident and not having clean underwear on. I wouldn't want you to embarrass yourself." My dad was in his late thirties, so I gathered he could work out the underoo situation, but hey, that's a Grandma Carol thing.

The hurts and oddities faded into the background for me with Grandma. I compartmentalized her challenging traits and idolized the accomplished woman she also was.

THE OLD FAMILY RECIPE · 27

I spent a lot of time at my grandparents' house, and there, life revolved around the mealtime rituals. To this day, I am hopeless when it comes to cooking and entertaining guests. I admire the gift of mastering a good meal and always looked up to Grandma Carol's incredible ability to throw a party. She was the consummate *hostess with the mostest*. She served cocktails promptly forty-five minutes before dinner was ready, even when it was only my grandparents and me. She'd have a Manhattan, or a Martini, and Grandpa would rotate between drinks I didn't recognize. Grandma would even whip up Shirley Temples (with extra cherries) for me so I could also partake in Happy Hour. I sipped the bubbly treat hiding the pinky that was ever so slightly raised up in classy celebration.

After cocktails, we headed back to the kitchen to put the finishing touches on dinner. I loved when she let me put the salad together. I made artistic designs with radishes and carrots atop the lettuce. Grandma always served the salad with Gardetti's Champagne Vinaigrette. Occasionally I wondered if there was champagne in it, but either way, it was delicious.

There was a normalcy to all this. One I didn't experience in my own home. I looked across the table while we silently chewed our food, and I felt *different*. Maybe I believed my grandparents "made it" in a way I didn't experience in other corners of my life. Maybe I was in awe of how a simple meal could transform into a work of art.

Grandma Carol loved us. Imagine a woman rushing out of the house at the sight of her grandbabies pulling into the driveway because she couldn't even wait the ten-second walk to the front door to wrap her arms around us and then squeeze our faces. Those hugs warmed my soul from the inside out. I would give anything for one more of those hugs.

Although Grandma may have been a bit on the shorter side, there was nothing small about her love. She happily shooed us into the house and into the living room. "Come in, come in. Say hello to your grandfather." Grandpa Bill would invariably be reading the daily newspaper in his leather chair in the corner of the room. He'd tilt the paper down, nod in our general direction and then lift it back up to keep reading.

We'd sit on the couch, and she would reach over and hold my hand while we all chatted. I can still feel the soft and leathery, wrinkled hand patting the top of mine. I hope I embody that part of Grandma Carol for my whole life. Even if metaphorically, I want to greet loved ones and chosen family at the door with a welcome hug. I want to sit with them, patting their hand and alternating between listening intently and small talk.

A firm belief backed her love that all her grandchildren would be quite accomplished. She checked in frequently about school and activities. She encouraged me to get involved with the community and volunteer. She was practical but also liked to have fun.

Grandma showed me you could make a career out of something you love. The symbol of her professional accomplishment sat on a desk in the corner of her room without a speck of dust on it. Her sewing machine was top of the line and well cared for. She took her hobby, talent, and ambition and made a raving success out of it in her life.

She showed me in real-time that I could start my own financial freedom journey. My financial success started in Grandma's mop closet and garden. My timecard was hung up on the refrigerator each time I came to stay with her. I earned $2 per hour for work inside and $4 per hour for work outside. The choice should have been easy—garden work because it made twice the money. Nope! Plants and I have a strict working agreement. We do not coexist. This left cleaning, and there was a lot of it. I was giddy watching the timecard fill after each day. I dutifully recorded my working time with a pencil and started doing mental math. Ca-ching.

I was proud to earn my own money. At the end of the week came my favorite day: payday. Inside my grandparents' room, there was a safe in the closet. Grandma would invite me into the bedroom. We walked over to the safe, and she opened it. Grandma pulled out a large stack of cash envelopes where my grandparents budgeted everything. She showed me, "See this one? It's for groceries. When the money runs out in our pay period, we get creative. That's possible, you know. Living in your means allows you to do more of what you really want to do."

Shuffling through the moderately thick envelopes, she pulled out one with two words written in her scrolled cursive with a black ballpoint pen. It read, "Frolic Fund."

"This one is my favorite," she said. "We use this one for all the fun stuff like movies and outings." She gave me a wink, took out my weekly pay from a different envelope, and put the puffy, white rectangles back to bed in the safe.

Later that day, I walked three blocks to the Seafirst Bank. I flashed my account card, smacked the twenty-dollar bill on the counter, and said, "All ones, please." The thick wad of one-dollar bills didn't even all fit in my wallet, so my back pocket swelled with the *booty*. I was a baller middle schooler. I was a millionaire and had the swagger to prove it. Work ethic equals money. Lesson learned. Money equals success. Got it.

For all her amazing traits, I was not naïve to the fact Grandma had issues. She drank too much, occasionally popped a prescribed pill, and could express herself with a temper so fiery, that my Uncle John called her "Sarge" and gifted her his military whistle. She stored it in the kitchen next to the cookie drawer.

I could see her flaws, but I adored her heart more. I love my version of Grandma Carol. She was the affable dingbat who gave up swearing for Lent and then said "shit" anyway. Then she would realize her mistake, "God damn it, I said shit. Oh shit, I said shit again." All this on day one of Lent.

I loved the way she loved my dad. The way she would brush off his stupid jokes, "Oh Jimmy. I don't understand your humor." The stories she would tell me about when he was little, his struggles at school, and how she momma-beared to get him access to what he needed to succeed. I want my legacy to be similar. I might be dingy and a little inappropriate, but I also want to be lovable and fiercely loyal.

Grandma was the best at everything in my eyes. I imagine her opinion of my adult choices, and it's still a huge marker of success for me. Do I love hard? Do I make space for the community at my proverbial table? Do I make people laugh? Am I true to who I really am? All these were important lessons I didn't know she was showing me while I trudged through my adolescence.

In my later teen years, the magic of Grandma Carol began to fade. Her several severe medical conditions caused her chronic pain. Walking became difficult due to ankle conditions, and she required frequent blood transfusions due to a rare blood disorder. She was fragile, less mobile, and needed more help. It was difficult for me to reconcile this new version of our matriarch with the Grandma Carol I grew up with.

I moved through high school and tried to spend whatever time I could with her, which admittedly became less and less. I was working too much and trying to keep up with the many responsibilities on my plate. This woman of fortitude was crumbling slowly in front of me, and I didn't handle it well. Ironically, I was throwing myself into things I believed she would approve of—three jobs and too many extracurriculars.

Life's clock kept ticking. My grandparents were older than most as they adopted my dad a bit later in life. They sold the house I essentially grew up in and moved into a small apartment. Their age and health meant the home had become a burden they couldn't keep up with anymore. I only visited the apartment twice. It was too painful to see them in the space. It was a picture of "one of these things is not like the other."

Soon after, Grandma's health began to fail even more, and they moved to a retirement facility—Grandma in the advanced care and Grandpa in the independent living section. Her mind slipped away, and dementia set in.

Looking back, I stretched out the unavoidable visits to avoid watching Grandma deteriorate. It would mean death was natural. I never witnessed the undoing of someone's life before, and this person wasn't just anyone. Grandma Carol represented a foundational piece of how I measured my achievement—her approval equated to success. I longed for her love and validation and worked my butt off to obtain it.

My string of excuses not to visit her stacked up high. Dad tried to get me to go to the nursing home, "She doesn't have much time, Riah." he said. Even at a young age, I knew the truth. I knew her dementia locked up memories of our late nights watching black and white shows, sharing recipes in the kitchen, or telling me life stories that passed long ago but were fresh to her.

The real Grandma Carol was already gone for me, and in truth, I was gone for her, too. I was lost somewhere where memories and loved ones hide when the mind decides to give up the ghost. I couldn't. I needed memories of *my grandma*, not the shell of who she was.

On February 6, 1997, Carol Dore Billington passed to the other side where no one would elbow her in the wooden pew when she fell asleep. She would slumber in peace in heaven for all eternity, perfectly healthy.

I was devastated and lost. How would I know if I was on the right track? Was all this hard work for waste? Grandma was the measuring stick for success, and I was going to have to stretch that measuring stick up to my full height of 5'8" and start to impress myself.

In the two years following her passing, I figured out how to live on my own and then graduated high school. I got married and then gave birth to my first baby—Angie would have been her first great-grandchild. There were many times I longed for her. I stumbled through what I was supposed to do. I still needed a firm hug and a warm hand pat, but the lessons she taught me didn't go away when she passed. Grandma was—and still is—alive and well in my heart.

Grandma Carol taught me even though life was messy, to do my best anyway. She showed me love could look like a drizzle of champagne vinaigrette on a bed of nutritious leafy greens or a swift elbow to the ribs to wake us up to life. Love can also cut like a knife without trying. I learned money could be fun, success measurable in our expression of affection, and—maybe my favorite—to never forget the value of a good frolic.

CHAPTER 4

Smokey Smokey, Diet Coke-y

At eighteen years old, my loneliness reigned supreme. My coping mechanisms for that loneliness included three things. One cost a fortune in gas, and the other two could cause cancer. Joyrides with my friends (whenever I wasn't grounded) were my favorite, followed closely by spending hours with those same friends drinking Diet Coke and smoking cigarettes.

As a teen, I often heard my opinion didn't matter and that I was wrong. Deep in my soul, I tried to cling to the truth I wanted, which was to have a high opinion of myself. I could only hold on to this minimal self-esteem for a while before the voice of insecurity rang out in my ears. It was loud and always sounded the same. *How can you be happy? You're a burden for anyone who bothers to give a shit about you. Your life was worthless before, and it's even more useless now.* Wherever I went, loneliness followed.

With one exception, Denny's Diner. In a white cloud of tobacco-scented friendship, my friends and I found sacred sanctuary from the bullshit of life in the dingy restaurant—and it was good. Everyone should have a Denny's Diner. Your version of Denny's could be the mall, a park bench, or sitting in your car for an hour while the radio is on, and you want the silence and the butt warmers. When life goes to shit, cling to whatever form your Denny's takes.

It was 1997, and smoking and nonsmoking sections still separated the restaurant. We always got carded and would proudly turn over our IDs with baby-faced photos. It was a rare occasion that I had been deemed "good enough" not to be grounded to the house. It had been a long time since I had let my hair down with my friends. It felt good that I decided, *Fuck it. If I'm as bad as they say, I'm going to be fucking bad.* My version of bad didn't include sex, drugs, and rock and roll, though. Okay—maybe a little rock and roll. It was cheesy, from the '80s, and it piped in through my car's tiny speakers.

"You're sure about this?" Jake asked me as he lit the cigarette for me. I nodded my head quickly, took a deep breath in, and held it. Exhale. Another deep breath in, keep it again. Exhale.

"Yup," I said to him as steadily as possible through clenched teeth. He pulled the lighter away from me and took a big drag off his cigarette. He inhaled most of it in one go and, with a flick of his wrist, blew most of it out through his nose with a *whoosh*. The rest lingered in the air around us for a few moments until I exhaled the smoke I'd been holding in. Jake smiled and waved his hand to the waitress. She came over with her notepad ready and took our orders: three diet cokes and three cheeseburgers. My head spun a little after that first drag. It was like a terrible head rush, except it didn't go away.

"This sucks," I said as I exhaled another puff of smoke.

"It's not that bad," he said with a laugh and a wink. "Chill out. It's not like your mother is disowning you or something."

The inside of my mouth felt like it was searing with pain. It wasn't long before Jake's words would become more than foreshadowing. I tipped my straw to my lips and slurped a large drink of the infamous magic elixir to try and soothe my throat.

"I think you guys are depressed," Jess said, looking back and forth between us as she took another drag off her cigarette. Jake and I both shook our heads.

"We don't have anything to be depressed about," I said. I took another sip and peered outside. I didn't want to think about the fact that my grandma had died the month before, or about school, work, and home. I didn't want to think about how I was overachieving everywhere, but no one noticed. Instead, I was trying hard to be there in the moment with my friends. I was hiding my sadness poorly, and it was right underneath the surface.

We were all sitting in the back, in a booth facing each other. We could see everyone's reactions as the day went on. I looked around and stretched my arms out in beautiful freedom. A mini groan that usually accompanies a good stretch escaped my lips. It was hard for me to believe that I was at the diner. I felt like I spent much of my time punished those days, so it was weird to be out of the hell house.

Mistaking my sadness about home for my other usual grief about my future, Jake tried to comfort me. "I don't want you getting too down about not heading off to college next year," he patted me on my shoulder. "We'll work hard, and before you know it—independence. This is another stepping-stone to getting out of the house and making something of yourself. I mean, no college kids go through this stuff."

"Yeah," I sighed and peered glumly at my reflection in the window. My hair was a mess, and there were dark circles under my eyes from lack of sleep. *Thanks for the reminder, Jake.* I didn't care about making something of myself with independence. I wanted to be one of those carefree college kids instead. I blinked in the sad reflection. I sure didn't look like much of anything. "I think you're right," I said to hopefully end that line of conversation.

"You know what would make me feel better?" Jess said as she crossed her arms and looked down at the table with a mischievous smile on her face. "If you guys paid for my cigarettes today." I chuckled. This was classic Jess. Jake rolled his eyes.

"Jess, Riah barely owns that beater of a car out there. We can't pay for your cigarettes."

"Well, you're going to have to do something," she said with a grin. I sipped the Diet Coke, and I felt myself perk up a little bit more. I couldn't help myself. A small smile started to form. Jess reached over and punched me in the shoulder.

"Don't get too happy," she said as I winced from the pain. "You still have to pay for my bill after this too." I looked outside, and the momentary smile faded as the lighthearted moment passed. Although the sun was beating brightly out, it wasn't doing anything to help me feel better.

"What were you smiling about?" Jake asked. I turned to look at him and Jess and felt a bit strange. We were in a crowded restaurant, and somehow, we felt alone in our own world. I looked at Jake. He was looking down at his hands, which were currently wrapped around a cup of some coffee or tea or something. He'd been fidgeting with it for most of the time we had sat here waiting on our food to come out. He had managed to spill it once on himself and once on me. I still had the wet spot on my pants. I hadn't complained because I knew Jake was covering up his own struggles. His home life wasn't awful, but it wasn't great. I saw his tension and felt a wave of compassion.

"I was smiling because we've got each other," I said as I gave his shoulder a quick pat. He smiled at me and turned to face Jess, who started rummaging around, looking for a Chapstick in the bottom of her purse.

The food arrived, piping hot from the kitchen we could see behind the counter. We stubbed out our cigarettes, wolfed down our food, and lingered as long as we could. We were safe here. Hell, even our regular server Cindy knew us by first name. She didn't mind that our tips weren't always large because we tipped her well any chance we could. On this day, Jake and I pooled our deeply creased single-dollar bills and counted out enough to cover our bill and give Cindy a couple of bucks.

"I think it's time to get out of here," Jake said.

"Yeah," Jess agreed as she also dropped some cash on the table for Cindy, and we all stood up. I felt my heart skip a little with mini-joy as we walked toward the exit. We pushed through the vinyl-padded double doors, and they closed softly behind us. Jess sprinted across the parking lot and shouted back at me, "I think it's about that time. Let's joyride!"

Joyriding wasn't anything salacious or dangerous. We usually listened to the scratchy radio or whatever cassettes I happened to have in the car. We were happy, loved, and safe. In the confines of my tiny vehicle, we found refuge from life for a little while.

We piled into my car and Jake leaned back in his seat and relaxed as I pulled us away from the restaurant. Jess took a cigarette out of her pack as she slid down in her seat. There was a flash of flame and then the inhalation sound as she took a deep drag. I could already smell the smoke filling the car.

"I wish that smoking didn't smell so damn good," Jake said as he took a whiff of the air. I grinned at them in the rearview mirror and nodded my head in agreement. I popped the Toto cassette tape into the deck, and the song "Africa" wafted out the windows right along with the smoke. Off we went. We made quick work getting out of town, then took our time getting lost alongside roads while singing and laughing at stupid jokes. Sooner than we wanted, we wound our way up toward the valley and, ultimately, our homes.

As an adult, there are nights when I close my eyes and wish myself back to that time and smoke-filled place. Not because I was happy then or want to go back to experience that life. Instead, I want to savor that taste again: the taste of believing deep in my heart that even though the world told me the complete opposite, there was a chance that life could be better than what I had. There still existed a weak heartbeat of hope I would be able to one day erase the havoc of my problematic life. I want to tell that version of me it will eventually turn out okay.

It isn't hard to want to transport myself to Denny's in 1997. The four greasy walls of that diner held sacred conversations around the corner booth with the scratched table. There were tear-filled moments and cackle laughs over the stupidest shit. There was rebellious joy in friendship amidst fear. There was camaraderie even though we spent 90 percent of our lives very alone. Success looked messy, but we were cocky enough at that age to spit in its face if it didn't turn out the way we wanted. It didn't matter our lives' paths would not be smooth because we were too poor, unloved, or ignored.

We were all stubborn enough to believe we could beat the hand life dealt us. If success is power, as some people believe, we were planting our wobbly stake in the ground and reclaiming our power. In my own muted way, I was trying to claim the control and power I could with this destructive behavior because there was not a lot of light or success elsewhere.

How do we start the conversations about not being okay? If you always feel like your troubles would, in turn, burden someone else, how do we relate to each other in these darker topics? How can people who care about us possibly connect their own pain with ours in empathy if no one says anything? Adversity and its counterpart aren't a straight shot, and they shouldn't be lived alone. There needs to be a normalizing of sharing what we are going through without making the other person feel dumped upon. I am grateful even with only my insular group of friends, I had a safe place where I felt I could reach beyond my current reality.

Ironically, I'm currently glancing over at a trusty can of Diet Coke that symbolizes a companion that has lasted throughout the years. Not lying, I love this beverage so much that I have a Diet Coke-themed mini-fridge in my home office that fits six cans. It's a funny mascot if you think about it. The soda's formula and ingredients are atrocious for your body. (Yes, you don't have to tell me what I already know. I have seen the video of the dude cleaning his car battery with a can of Diet Coke. I don't fucking care. It's delicious. Mmmmm... clean that internal battery acid.) But one little sip and I'm back to simpler hard times.

Your Denny's Diner may have been a cafeteria or the kitchen at a friend's house. Another location from my past that brings me the same emotional memories was the roof of my best friend's house. We would sit out there for hours looking at the stars, bullshitting about everything and nothing all at once. Find your sanctuary. Find the shit that makes you happy. Find the simple in the hard times. Find that fleeting hope again.

I cordially invite you to take a trip down your own memory lane. What's your memory mascot of when you had a quiet revolution? Is it Alanis Morrisette's "You Oughta Know" turned up to volume eight while cruising five mph over the speed limit on the freeway? Is it a leather jacket way back in the closet with safety pins all over the lapels? Whatever it is, cling to that. Hard. Sometimes life is a vicious bitch, and we all need a little joy in the madness.

I lift my delicious Diet Cokey with your glass of goodness and salute our achievement.

CHAPTER 5

The Girl in the Car

Life begins for people at different milestones. This might be when you walk onto your school's campus for the first time, when you marry the one you love, or even when you finally accept a path you were on is no longer serving you.

Many things change after we are eighteen years old. Life should unfold and be a predictable series of beginnings. Unfortunately, I was pushed into the next stage of life without notice.

There was no fight or drama in the house the night my life turned upside down. In fact, I wasn't even home when they made the decision. I got a beep on my beat-up teal pager. I pulled over to a payphone and called home. "We need to talk," my mom said grimly.

"What's up?" I replied, totally clueless. I was used to being in trouble, but I didn't know what I did this time. She didn't really answer, so I asked again, "What's up?" She only directed me to come home.

I unlocked the door and walked to my room at the end of the hall. I didn't leave my purse or my belongings in the living room because it wasn't allowed. The house was quiet. I knew my sister was likely staying out of the way, reading a book or journaling in her room. I didn't seek my mom out because I knew she would come to me, and she did. She didn't even enter my room. My mom stood in the doorway and stoically told me I needed to pack all my belongings and move out within the week. My mouth opened in utter shock even though I should have seen this coming a mile away.

I had a plan to move out two weeks after graduation because life with my mom and her husband had been challenging for years. My move out timeline should have been plenty soon enough for them. Unfortunately, not. My ears felt fuzzy as I watched the words come out of her mouth in slow motion. It started to sink in. I was no longer welcome to live there, although there were still three months before I finished high school. *What the fuck was happening?* Although I was eighteen, I was still a child. I wasn't ready to launch. There were too many logistics to figure out still. I had sketched out my rough plan because I knew I had to fly out of there before it got worse, but none of the details were in place.

I wasn't desperate to stay in a toxic environment where I received daily reminders of what a burden I was. Over the years, they told me how intolerable I was again and again. However, living there was a necessity until my education was complete. But I guess not. Apparently, I wouldn't have that luxury. *Noted. Figure it all out on your own, Riah.*

My brain drifted briefly to distract from the catastrophe happening in front of me. I remembered the one time I tried to quietly communicate to my mother how hated I felt in the house. She didn't look me in the eyes and simply said, "Riah. Don't start." We were standing in the kitchen. I was doing the dishes, and she was making dinner. My gaze fell straight to my hands, defeated. Reaching out had been an emotional risk. I knew chances were I would face rejection, and there it was.

My needs were invalid and unacceptable.

Snap back. Enough of that memory. My focus came back to my bedroom and the situation at hand. I begged for answers. I was anxious and confused. "Why? Why? What happened?" I already knew I wasn't welcome or wanted there, but the timing was off. There was no fight, no disobedience. No words exchanged, no misbehavior. My mom just stood there and repeated herself, clutching her hands in front of her.

"You have a week to move out. Clear out this room and take your stuff with you."

Even twenty-five years later, I still can't comprehend what I could have done to warrant turning me out into the streets. I wasn't perfect, but seriously? Have you met a teenager who is? I was a kid who felt beaten down, defeated, and angry. I walked around daily with a chip on my shoulder, profoundly sad and self-loathing. I felt like the biggest piece of shit, worthless because the person who was supposed to love me the most didn't love me at all.

There we were, in my bedroom, at an impasse. At some point, since she wasn't going to tell me why this was happening and I wouldn't stop asking, Mom retreated to her side of the house with her husband. With no other option, I quickly moved into triage mode. I needed to figure out my practical needs because I couldn't comprehend the emotional train wreck I was experiencing. I would come back later for my stuff. I wanted to get the hell out of there.

Oh, sweet Jesus, my little sister. Because I wrapped myself up in what was happening to me, I forgot she was in the adjacent room. We had been in this warzone together and leaving her made my heart ache with worry. She was only thirteen, and even though she had already caught major flak from the adults in the house, I knew everything would fall on her shoulders in my absence, and she was such a tender soul. Her greatest desire was love and acceptance. This was horrific.

Frantically, I wrote her a letter telling her not to take shit from anyone, not even our parents. I told her what they said was lies. I told her she was worthy and beautiful. Recently, she told me she still has that letter stashed away. Part of me wants to read it, however, most of me knows I'm not strong enough to see the chicken scratch of a young person during the worst distress of her life.

The first night, there was no time to figure out what was next. I hastily grabbed a few things, threw them in a backpack, and headed to my car. I can't remember where exactly I drove to. I ended up in an empty parking lot, parked the car, and sat still.

My wipers were old and streaked across the windshield while making an annoying noise. *Hiss. Hiss. Pause. Hiss. Hiss. Pause.* I sat staring ahead blindly. Life sent me this metaphorical flat tire and stranded me without a spare. Shit, I didn't even have a life-hack-jack. I sat for a long time. *Hiss. Hiss. Pause. Hiss. Hiss. Pause.* My hands firmly gripped the steering wheel at ten and two. I was all amped up with nowhere to go.

There were only a few options and none of them were ideal. One was to sit there in the parking lot and do nothing. I could stay in my car and turn the heat on. I could try to chill out. I mean, when life pukes, sometimes you've got to sit in it for a while until things cool down. Drinking anything alcoholic—my normal escape from nights when my heart hurt from reality—held no appeal to me.

I was numb, lost, and my chest ached with an emotion I couldn't put my finger on. Emptiness? I squeezed my eyes tight until they hurt. I imagined my heart cracked open, with dark, dusty soot sitting inside. There was no life left, no joy, no understanding of where I fit in because the last shred of my safety net was yanked painfully from underneath. *Maybe this is what I deserve. Maybe I AM a piece of shit.*

Sitting there wouldn't move the needle in this situation. I was stuck. I glanced out the driver's side window, and the rain made skinny ribbons as they streamed down the glass, swaying in a sad dance. Even the sky cried for my pain. *I definitely can't cry harder than the rain—but it seemed the sky was no competition for the tears that wouldn't stop.* My future fell through those fingers gripping the steering wheel tightly.

I painfully wished for someone to be with me in the passenger seat. I longed for a dear friend or anyone who could take away the loneliness and tell me how to move forward. Instead, the passenger seat taunted me with its emptiness. Aside from my CD holder case, an empty Diet Coke can, and a random lip gloss, the seat was unoccupied. None of those items would offer much comfort. I shut the ignition off.

How do we course correct? Success in this situation for me—for us—looked like moving in any direction except here. We have to pick something small and start somewhere. We have to move. We have to do something.

I chose to go for a walk.

The rain picked up, and my hair soaked in minutes. I was already letting the tears do their thing, and I looked terrible at that point. My hair plastered to my face. All I could see out of either eye was a partial vision of the blurry, gray world. I pulled my hoodie on and kept plodding along. I tried to ignore my crying, but there was no ignoring it. Wails escaped and I prayed the rain would cover the sound. The tears streamed down my face, slowly covering my nose, which had snot running out of both nostrils. It was gross. What did I expect when I'd spent months building up a solid head of steam?

When I'd been hot-headed angry at the injustice of my life but unable to say a word?

I endured a lot in the last few years in that house. But I kept my mouth shut. I slid in right before curfew every night so I wouldn't bother them with my presence, but I also didn't get punished for breaking the rules. I did everything they asked to make it to graduation day and for what? It all came crumbling down anyway. *Stupid. Stupid. Stupid.*

I was miserable with no idea where to go. I considered calling someone but quickly dismissed the idea. It seemed such a heavy conversation to have. What would I even say? I couldn't call someone up at 10:30 p.m. at night and tell them, "Hey, guess what? My life is fucked." It was embarrassing. Would they think I did something wrong? I couldn't emotionally afford another rejection in one evening. Instead, I chose to weather the night alone.

Move Riah. While walking, I ran through all the options. Which would hurt the least? I was determined to keep this situation under wraps. I was embarrassed. I didn't want to get into it with anyone or rehash the situation. It was too painful. Most of all, if I asked any of my friends and their parents rejected me too, I might have gone straight up suicidal. I adored them too much and I physically, emotionally, and spiritually could not make it through one more adult turning me away. I was on the brink and wasn't trying to take any risks.

My go-to *would* have been Grandma Carol's house and enrolling in finishing high school at the community college. Sadly, she passed away a mere two or three months before that night. My dad also would have absolutely taken me in, but it was impractical in a million ways, and I couldn't stomach being a burden to him.

Fuck being stuck. I could work this out. You can't make it work for you if you don't try, right? *What next?* First, I could stop crying. I aggressively wiped my face dry with the sleeve of my hoodie. I kept thinking until I started to make sense of my next steps. Although I wasn't ready to act on it, there was a plan brewing.

Eventually, my walk brought me back to the Party Mobile, my tan 1983 Nissan Stanza hatchback that would be my not-so-sweet digs for the next few days while I worked things out. I unlocked the driver's side, sat, and slid the seat all the way back. I pulled my hoodie strings tight. I covered my swollen eyes to block out the streetlights. Sleep wasn't going to come easy. Still, I would try.

It took a few nights of numbly existing during the daylight hours and sleeping restlessly in my car, but I remembered the Johnson family. They were low risk. I didn't know them well, but they knew my home life was problematic and once flippantly offered me a place to crash if I needed it in the future.

I prayed for the sun to come up. No amount of tossing and turning in the driver's seat would make it comfortable, and my heart wasn't the only thing that was sore. There was a half-baked plan, and I needed to see it through. On the third day, at 7:00 a.m. on the dot, I showed up on the Johnsons' doorstep. Mrs. Johnson slowly opened the door, surprised. I hastily and self-consciously explained my situation, and she ushered me into the warm living room.

Several days later, I returned to my mom's house to collect the last of my things. The house was quiet and echoed my sadness while I moved between my room and the car. Aside from packing anything not marked for garbage or donation, I wasn't sure what to do with what was left. There was the matter of the unintentional collection of half-empty liquor bottles. I lined them up one by one as I dug them out from underneath my bed. After some effort, the glass bottles stood like sad soldiers on the top of the closet shelf. I couldn't control this situation. I *could* make a statement. Even though I am sure the bottles gave the impression that I was a crazed, alcoholic teenager, each bottle represented a series of nights too painful to stay mentally awake for.

On those awful nights, I listened to offensive music, wrote in my journal, or laid in my uncomfortable bed. I stared at the ceiling, pausing periodically to swig from the bottle. It didn't matter what was in it—whiskey, tequila, vodka, rum. I would drink whatever I could buy from the girl down the street who sold me partially consumed bottles. Her price markup was incredibly steep. With her early start, I am sure she's an amazing entrepreneur by now. I didn't drink nightly. But on the really loud nights or the ones where I was called names, and no one would defend me—those nights called for being numb. I used the bottles to quiet the pain of a broken heart.

I wished to call a friend, but I couldn't because, in a fit of rage one night, they ripped the phone out of my wall. The torn section where the socket had been taunted me by the door. I was alone. I was in pain. I needed out of my reality. This happened over several years and the bottles accumulated. I couldn't get rid of them. Where would I throw them away without getting caught? No solution appeared, so I stashed them under the bed in my horrifically messy room.

To someone else, these bottles may have looked like confirmation of all they would say about me, before and after I was made to leave. I was bad. I deserved punishment. I misbehaved despite my efforts to win affection through my superior academics and dogged work ethic. Instead, the bottles were the message I hadn't revealed. They whispered: *This* is the monument to my years of sadness and to my inability to receive love here. *I hoped I was wrong, and someday you would love me. I needed protection and to experience the childhood I deserved. Unfortunately, my wishes were as empty as these.*

I stood for a few moments in my now untenanted bedroom and stared at them at the top of my closet and counted: *one, two, three, four, five...* the list was long. Then I started at the beginning and counted again with the true metric: *rejection, lack of recognition, ignoring my needs, neglect, abuse of power, then pain, pain, pain, pain...*

I was reclaiming the voice they stole from me at sixteen years old and thought I was *showing them*. But when I look back, my heart weeps for a broken child who, for many nights, the bottle was her only companion. Leaving the bottles wasn't a rebellion. It was a sad goodbye to the childhood I didn't have.

I remember this parting moment clearly: all the ages and versions of me turning away and walking out of the blue box of a house.

We were saying a final goodbye to my home of eighteen years. We walked away from running carefree as a little girl in the backyard, playing on the mostly broken swing set, and making my little sister eat slugs. I walked away from the old days sitting on the bathroom counter while Daddy played guitar and sang gospel songs in full voice volume while performing to the big mirror above the vanity.

No more music for this soul. I said goodbye to the tiniest shred of innocence from my early teen years before all the life in between then and the life I would have later. I slung my backpack onto my shoulder. I clung to my heart's resilience and let my soul break into pieces. I silently let the tears soak my face.

I am not alone in this not-so-joy-ride. We bang our hands on the steering wheel in vain and let out screams of frustration.

The going is going to get tough, you're in bumper-to-bumper traffic, and the windshield is blurry from rain and tears. The only exit for the next hundred miles is blocked off because, of course, they're doing construction on it today of all days. You have to admit you can't keep going like this. You have to pull over onto the shoulder to take a break, dry your eyes, and change the radio station. Breathe deep. Fill your chest until it might burst, then exhale all the bullshit you have absolutely no control of. Pick yourself back up.

This experience created the most horrific scar on my soul. It has healed enough that it's no longer a gaping wound. Still, it's definitely there—hiding under the surface. I've worked through adversity, and most of the time, that's enough. Only, I'm in my forties now, and most of the time, I feel stronger, finally able to put to bed what happened. Then something will trigger a memory. I am taken right back there, to that life-altering night, gripping the wheel and wondering why my own mother doesn't love me? Why was I tossed away so easily?

When I think about the girl in the car, I imagine I am sitting next to this younger version of me. I've gently pushed the other stuff from the passenger seat onto the floor to clear a space and I sit down. She doesn't look in my direction. She knows I am there. She stares straight ahead, silently dying inside while staring out a dirty windshield.

I look over at her fresh skin, her curly hair, and her demeanor and feel the deepest grief. Only a few short hours before that phone call from mom, her day was full of hope. Now she's lost. She's grasping for clarity. *Baby, there won't be clarity from this situation.* It's twenty-five years later, and I still don't understand it. Imagining her in this car still makes the tears well up in my eyes. I motion for her to lay her head in my admittedly more ample lap. She breaks down, and I stroke her hair while her body wracks with sobs.

We sit like this for a long time. She cries so violently. I think she may throw up. I let her get it out. No one else is there to hold her at this moment—technically, she's alone. So, I see me leaning in to close the gap and to bring her closer to me. I do my best to wrap my arms around her broken little soul. "It's okay," I croon softly into her delicate ear with gold hooped earrings. "I've got you, and we can do this. We're not done."

There is time and space for more healing.

CHAPTER 6

The Tassel Was Worth the Hassle

I have had a sordid relationship (*cough cough* obsession) with college almost all my life. Even last night, I debated the pros and cons of a master's program after this book finds its way into the world. Do I need a master's to navigate through running an international business? Absolutely not. Do I want the perceived prestige and personal affirmation it will afford me? Absolutely yes. What I lacked in a legacy of monetary wealth growing up, I hoped I could make up for in a legacy of educational wealth.

This whole mission to achieve a degree started when I was eleven years old. One summer, I was staying over at my grandparents' house for the week, and Grandma Carol and I were sitting at the breakfast bar, eating oatmeal with brown sugar, raspberries, blueberries, and strawberries. It was essentially a bowl of fresh ingredients with a touch of oatmeal. I clearly remember the old German grandfather clock ticking and tocking in the background when she turned to me. After sleepy small talk, the topic shifted to Grandma's educational story.

"When I was growing up, higher education was rare for girls," she said. "I am fortunate my parents supported me and sent me to the university."

Grandma explained when she was a young girl, all most women could aspire to be were successful housewives in a wealthy family. In other words, Grandma Carol's educational background was unusual.

"Even though I came from Minnesota, not near the fashion business, I studied and honed my skills. I received a diploma, which makes me happy because before meeting your grandfather, I built a successful fashion career despite coming from outside of the industry."

We moved the conversation down the narrow stairs, past the laundry room, and out to the garage, where huge cabinets housed trinkets, photos, and treasures from adventures with Grandpa. There, way in the back, were worn albums in an equally worn box.

"These were my designs that were in Nordstrom's and other stores." She rattled off a list I am sure was impressive. We took the album back upstairs to look closer. Grandma explained how she moved out to Washington to further her career and live with her brother, who was a well-known dentist. She met Sherod Billington, a much older pediatrician who had a stable medical practice, a prolific presence in the educational community of the University of Washington, and soon, her promise to marry him. Despite the career she worked hard to build up, the real title she desired was "Mom."

Once my grandparents were married, they tried for many years to have kids biologically. For many reasons, they pursued adoption. First came my Aunt Laurie and then my father, James. She poured her education, life experience, and energy into her children instead of for customers and then later into her grandchildren.

Grandma Carol said, "Riah, you may look at me and believe college was a waste of my time—it wasn't. I learned about life there. I learned more about who I was and what I am capable of. It was one of the singular most important things I did."

She continued, "I want you to know it's crucial you go to college because you will need it in your life too. Life teaches you things when you are young, and you may need the extra help. You go to college, and you get a degree. I don't care what your degree is in. Find the degree and career that meets your needs. I want you to know education is crucial. It was for me, and it will be for you. You are bright, I can see it, and this will serve you well for the rest of your life."

She told me should I choose the life of a housewife. It would be fine. Be a housewife with a bachelor's degree. It's that important. She assured me if I got good grades, she and my grandpa would help me with college.

"Okay, I promise." I tucked that promise in my heart for good.

Even though I didn't know what "help me with college" meant in terms of dollars and cents, I knew "help me" meant it would be possible. With this assurance in my heart, I set my eyes firmly on the goal and tried my hardest to get the best grades on the planet and get accepted into an amazing school.

My freshman year is when things became crystal clear for me. Even though college was always a "duh, obviously!" for me, I didn't know what career I would explore. Enter the career report. Freshmen crowded the career center to take our career assessment. It was a heady cocktail of hormones, gangly limbs, braces, and pimples. We looked at the teacher expectantly like we were to receive a tarot reading that would predict our futures with utmost accuracy. The assignment was clear: take the assessment, choose a career, and then research everything we could, using the resources in the room. We would later take the research back to the classroom to start our reports. I took the assessment, taking my time, lest I answer incorrectly and be stuck forever in a career I hated. The result was a list of ten different options.

I opened the resources for several of them but, after a bit, stumbled upon the option that was one hundred percent right for me: I was going to be a physical therapist! The average amount of money they could make floored me—$40,000 a year! *That's what I am talking about!* I couldn't even imagine that amount of money. It may seem laughable now, however, at the time, the minimum wage was a measly $4.25. I kept reading the report. Stop the presses! Physical therapists could work four days a week and have an assistant who does the heavy lifting? *Dang, they're making bank and working one day fewer than everyone else? Hell yeah. Sign me up.*

The summer between my sophomore and senior year, I discovered the University of Puget Sound in Tacoma. I toured this college while at Drill Team camp one summer and instantly knew it was the place for me. We stayed in the dorms. I ate with my friends in the cafeteria and wandered through the campus full of grass and trees and secretly pretended I was a student there.

For the first time in my life, I could see my future. My shoulders pushed a little further back, and I stood a little taller. It was a private college with a beautiful campus that specialized in physical and occupational therapy. There was only one issue—Grandma Carol passed away several months ago, and the cost of her end-of-life care was much more than my grandparents had bargained for. So how was I going to pay for everything?

Then things started falling apart in my junior year of high school. I took a rigorous course of studies—almost all AP and Honors. Junior year was the only year I could choose fun things for my electives, but instead, I chose Trigonometry, Marine Biology, and Physics. I was determined to have the most competitive application. Even though I had no intention of joining the military, I took the ASVAB for fun and the PSATs to get prepared. I worked three jobs and participated in Drill Team, Diversity Club, and other extracurricular groups. School was tiring but going okay overall. However, things at home were not great.

I had no support for my goals, and others frequently reminded me I would be a fool to believe I could achieve them. My grades started slipping. My heart didn't leap when I imagined my future anymore. There was only a desperate ache for a dream hanging on by the thinnest of threads. Maybe my naysayers were right. Maybe this was impossible. Where was the money going to come from? Who would give me a scholarship? Could I even do this alone if I didn't have moral support at home? My dad believed in me, but we didn't live together anymore.

My senior year fared much the same. I had the chance to earn college credit in my Advanced Placement English class but no personal money to pay for the reduced tuition. I drifted through the year, barely existing. My body was still doing all the activities, still working, and still occasionally hanging out with friends. I usually wasn't allowed to go anywhere outside of work, so I spent most of my time in my room at home. My mind was stuck.

Life became a blur: I got up, put on the least dirty article of clothing, went to school, pretended to hear the lesson, and fell asleep in class because the nightmares and numbness kept me up at night. My teachers noticed, and I had to tell them what was going on, but I told no one else. Not even people who would have considered themselves good or best friends at school. I didn't want pity or judgment. I didn't want to recount the story of being rejected on such a visceral level. I didn't want any of this situation. I floated through the halls in a daze until a bell rang and I was free. Free to drive myself to job number two, which paid my rent and provided dinner for the night.

While adults at school knew things were challenging, no one told me the educational options I might have. No one told me how to pay for college when you aren't wealthy but aren't quite poor enough. No one knew how to help a deeply hurting young woman who was on the brink of homelessness.

My peers were living their dreams. They arranged their dorm rooms and even requested a bestie for their roommate. They were planning adventures of out-of-state colleges or European gap years. Meanwhile, I was putting one pathetic foot in front of the other. Somewhere deep inside, I recognized there might have been choices, but they all involved risk. The risk was an untenable factor in my life because my psyche could not handle rejection one more time—not from a person, a college, a scholarship, or even a job. I simply could not handle any more hopes dashed or any more anticipation of a good thing with any possibility of being taken away. I was numb. I was safe only within myself. I was lost.

Graduating from high school almost didn't happen. I still had a detailed research paper due. Ms. Whitman—*God bless her*—had taken mercy on me and extended my deadline to graduation day. Now, kids, we didn't have Google or YouTube back then. Students had to visit nearby research libraries, look up books on our topics, and make photocopies. I stayed up all night working on the paper. I took way too many NoDoz pills and drowned them with black coffee and Diet Coke. In the end, I wrote all fifteen pages of my research paper by hand. The plan was to hit the school early and commandeer one of the word processors in the library. The requirement was to submit the paper in twelve-point font, double-spaced, with a bibliography in MLA format. No citation generator, folks! In a rush to get to school early, a critical error happened. Somewhere on the road from here to there, I lost the paper. I called my house to see if it was there. Nope. I dumped my backpack out and sorted through every scrap even though my fifteen 8.5 x 11 sheets of paper weren't visible. I cried in frustration. I walked down the hall to Ms. Whitman's room to see what I could do.

She shook her head sadly. Her choppy, endearing German accent confirmed my fear: "I have already made many exceptions, Riah. You must turn it in today, or I have no other option than to give you a failing grade."

I walked out of the classroom, my back hit the hallway wall, and I slid down into a sitting position. I cradled my knees with my head bowed and my curly hair like curtains hiding my shame. Sobs racked my body. The bell rang, and the halls filled. I was beyond the point of caring. I cried until I dry heaved. Students stepped over me and kept heading to their classes. My friend, Sydney, walked past, and it took her a second to realize it was me. She pulled me up by the elbow. I stood and shirked her off, openly crying for the whole school to see.

Through the hiccups, starts, and stops, she was able to piece together what had happened. Sydney was one of the few who knew my situation because it was Sydney's family who took me in. She literally pushed me with two hands on my back into the library again and sat me down in front of the word processor.

She lifted my hands and put them on the keyboard. "Write, Riah. Everything is in your head. You studied this. You know this."

"I can't," I pleaded. I truly believed it was all over. Getting a GED was my only option, and those who doubted me and said I would amount to nothing were right.

"You have no choice," she said.

Magically, one finger moved. Then another. More and more information spilled out of my brain, through my heart, then my arms, then my fingers, and then the clickety-clack of the keyboard. The screen filled slowly with words.

I pulled it out of my ass, and I did write the paper. I got an A.

Still, college was off the table for me, and I spent the next year working menial job after menial job. I wondered if my life would always be working retail in a mall for grumpy ass people or taking orders with a too dirty apron. I wanted something stable, and this lifestyle was always on the brink of having hours cut or someone getting irritated and threatening my job.

So instead of getting a college degree, I married at nineteen. It was a choice of family over education. I sat with the choice for several years. I had my first baby when I was twenty years old. I had my second child at twenty-two, but the desire for education was still inside me. We had little money. When my second child was under a year old, I decided to see how I could dip my toe back into school. I ended up signing up for a noncredit Spanish class. It would help me because my husband's family only spoke Spanish at the time, and while I had an interest in learning the language, I was nowhere near proficient in it. I knew the course would improve my fluency, *and* it would fulfill my desire for education.

I studied as if I was getting credit for the class. The teacher bumped me up in class level—twice. I protested, knowing my speaking ability was not on the same level as my reading and writing skills, but she said my speaking Spanish was great and grammar and writing would follow soon behind. I felt like my tiny spark of a pilot light that was lit at eleven years old was doused with gasoline. I wanted to go back to school. However, the logistics were challenging. I needed to work, tend to two babies under two, and had no regular childcare.

I plotted and schemed. *I still have this desire for a reason.* I reasoned with myself. I visited the local community college office and did the research to see how I could make it happen. I found out there was a program they offered, allowing students to make three tuition payments over the course of the quarter. After having my lifelong dream tossed aside, I was thrilled. This was the answer.

I began going one class at a time. One math class, then one English class, then one history class, then one statistics class. I had the map of what I needed for my degree, and I only took classes on said map. Money was tight, and I was making a choice to sacrifice other things to do this.

It took me seven long years to get my two-year associate degree. I didn't take breaks. I studied four quarters per year—one quarter after another. People would say to me, "You're crazy. Why are you doing this? It's taking such a long time. I would have given up. How can you handle all this?"

With a tired sigh, I would say, "I just do."

Even though I knew my life was suffering in other areas, I made a promise to myself to finish. I was going to make good on it. After graduating from community college, I decided I did not want to walk in the graduation ceremony, and I was going to save the experience. I was only going to consider going to commencement when I got my bachelor's degree.

At this point, I had gotten smart. Instead of salary wages, when I had a job review, I negotiated to have my employer pay my college tuition. This was beneficial for both of us. I was studying things applicable to my administrative jobs, and it was a tax write-off for my employer as an educational experience for an employee. (This is an actual option, little ones!)

I survived eons of endless studying, momming hard, sleeping only a little, and growing my budding career in leadership. I loved it even though it almost killed me because it was challenging to manage all my personal, professional, and educational commitments while exhausted. I advanced in my career quickly, and working additional hours meant I had to shift to online classes.

I got pregnant with my third child near the end of earning my degree, and I decided I would go all the way through anyway, and I only took off one quarter—the quarter Gabriela was born. My grades suffered. However, I was still determined to keep going. Maybe I wouldn't have a 4.0, but I was going to finish.

I increased my course load from one class to full-time, on top of working sixty–seventy-hour weeks and managing three children. It was insanity. It didn't matter. I was doing it—I was getting my degree.

At last, I completed the checklist. I met all the requirements, and I was ready to apply for graduation. There was a hiccup. Because I was determined to stay in line with which classes were required for the degree, I only took the degree-specific classes, so I was three credits short on electives.

I signed up for an online orientation for a college course worth one credit and a weekend stress management course worth two credits. Heh. The irony of stress management being my last college class...

I did it. I was finally completing this process after a total of twelve years instead of the typical four. I realized the end of a decades-long pact with a woman who had passed away many years before. I wish Grandma Carol could have been there with me. I wish she had waved from the crowd with a big smile on her face. She would say to the people in the stands next to her, "See her? The pretty one in the fourteenth row, three seats in? She's my granddaughter!" Who knows? Maybe she was with me in spirit.

On graduation day, I found myself alone in full regalia in the back staging area. Because my program was small, the college lumped our group together with the School of Professional Services with all the teachers who studied in cohorts for years. They were all excited, giggling and laughing together. There were hugs and congratulations and smiles. In stark comparison, I stood shifting from one foot to the other while my cap balanced precariously on my head and my honor cords swayed back and forth over my honors stole.

Any awkwardness melted away when a lot of yelling told us to get moving.

"*Line up!*"

I didn't know which line to stand in. I picked one from the two options and hoped for the best.

The stadium was large; I wasn't sure if my family would be able to see me. I emerged from the back area and discovered not only could they see me, but the line was also in front of my family, right down to the row I was in! There they were: my husband, my three children, my parents, (with whom I finally reconciled), my siblings, my friends, and everyone who had sacrificed on my behalf to make the day possible. They were there to support and love me. I waved and smiled, and they mirrored those motions back to me.

There were the happiest of tears. These were "I achieved the seemingly impossible" tears. I put my hands in my lap and fidgeted with them in anticipation. I could barely focus on what the speakers were saying. I'm sure it was inspirational as shit, but I was busy being transported back to when I was a teenager, walking the University campus for the first time with a dream in my heart and a spring in my step. My heart raced a little. My shoulders rolled back. My chin lifted a bit. I made it happen despite all the obstacles.

The moment finally arrived. Someone called my name, "Amariah Grace Gonzalez, Bachelor of Science in Administrative Management and Information Technology." Someone strange to me handed me my degree, and we paused for the obligatory photo. Before I knew it, I was stepping off the stage. Even though they still called out names, the ceremony was complete for me. When prompted, I crossed the tassel from left to right, moving me from all I had wished for into my limitless future.

If you want something, you *really* have to want it. You have to want it past exhaustion, past any jealousy or inequity, past missing out on other important things.

Success is within your grasp. You may just need really long arms.

CHAPTER 7

Blend or Ascend

When was the last time you felt *enough*? Maybe it was when you were little, spinning in circles outside with your hands spread so wide that you thought you could embrace the whole world. Maybe it was the time your grandpa slyly slipped you a few dollars with a wink and a smile. Were you enough then?

I wasn't the little girl who twirled with my arms open wide. Those who know me now with my loud-mouth style, my cackle laugh, and boisterous attitude may be shocked to know I was a painfully shy child. It's true! Some of my earliest memories are bursting into tears when people would laugh in conversation when I was in the room. I automatically assumed it meant they were laughing at me. And so began my painful childhood, always wondering who was looking at me, who was judging me, if I would have a chance to fit in, and I convinced myself I knew the answer to that already—no.

From my early experiences, it was clear I was looking for something that would complete me. I sought external validation because when I looked inside, I felt subpar. The search for *enough* didn't stop in the super early years. In elementary school, I struggled to fit in and longed to have lots of friends. I aligned myself with a super alpha *best friend* because I was too shy or chickenshit to make my own decisions. What if I made the wrong choice and even more people didn't like me?

I was in second grade when I realized my family didn't have money. Although our basic needs were met at home, there wasn't a ton of disposable income for things like name-brand clothing or other crap the cool kids had that made them worthy of all the attention. The style at the time was leggings with stacked neon socks, side ponytails with crimped hair, Hammer pants, and ripped jeans. Man, it was those ripped jeans that got me. I was so proud to wear them to school because I worked hard on them. I spent the better part of one Sunday preparing my fashion masterpiece—cutting and then lovingly shredding the threads to match the style. My mom caught me mid-process, "Why would you take a perfectly good pair of school pants and destroy them?" It was too late, though. The genius damage had already been done.

Let's be clear. I gave two shits about this fashion trend. Really, I could not have cared less. What I desperately wanted was acceptance, assimilation, and conformity. At the beginning of the school year, the Queen Bee of our class approached me with a haughty, "Where do you shop for school clothes, anyway? *Goodwill?*"

"Uh... no?" I tried to deny it. It was then I truly discovered that secondhand clothing was different... and different meant bad. Noted.

I didn't have the crimped side ponytail. I didn't have the cool turtlenecks or puffy jackets. Hell, I didn't even have the neon socks to wear in tandem pairs to accent my delicate eight-year-old ankles. I did have these ridiculous jeans, and they were my ticket into breaking into the popular crowd: The Preps. The Preps were an elite group of kids who did have it all: perfect hair, perfect families, money to do all the optional school activities, and unspoken rules over the playground and the classroom. They got the lead roles in plays and were elected Student Body President or Student Class Representative. I wanted a slice of their life.

I knew that being who I was would never fly. The few times I tried, even my one steady friend would make fun of me. I was unlikeable and needed desperately to blend in—nothing out of the ordinary for this chickadee.

Monday morning came, and aside from dealing with the disapproval from my mom, I was allowed to go to school with my jeans creation. Like clockwork, Queen Bee aggressively approached me with her perfect teeth and stupidly perfect *everything*.

"Hey Riah," she called out in a sing-song voice while already chuckling. "Did you make those jeans yourself or something? They are *sooooooo* ugly!" Her posse of followers snickered behind her.

I vehemently denied the accusation and died inside realizing I would have to spend the next six hours in these jeans. After throwing my "masterpiece" in the garbage that night, I made a pact with myself to try hard not to show my feelings. I would stick with the status quo in every way I could control. It was an impossible task but one I was committed to doing.

Until the following days, when someone would point something out or pick on me (or breathe in my direction), I would start crying. I was—and still am—a total crybaby. I wear my emotions on my sleeve, and they all come out in tears. Anger? Tears. Joy? Tears. Fear and shame? Tears and tears. This made me the butt of many jokes and perpetuated my unpopular status through the years. It's hard to blend in with the crowd when you are too busy crying about how much you don't. I learned to despise my vulnerability. It was my greatest weakness, and I wished it away whenever I could. Alas, I would inevitably feel something, and the tears would come.

Wipe those tears dry and work on blending in. Crybabies aren't given the attention they need. The years passed. I buried those tears in accomplishments. I became the teacher's pet. I earned excellent grades and high test scores. I wanted societal, parental, and academic approval. Above all, I wanted to fly a bit under the radar. Garner enough attention that the little emotional cup filled halfway, but not so much that someone will kick it over. Blend, Riah, blend.

It wasn't until my 30s that my friend, Katherine, taught me the importance of the word *bold*. She wielded it as a hilariously catty comment, spoken in hushed tones, "Well, that's a bold choice, isn't it?" But it could also be affirmative.

Katherine was the master of assembling an outfit. Things that I *would never* have thought to mix and match, she pulled off and looked like a movie star. I asked her how she did it. How did she make gold dinosaur cardigan clips look so chic?

"Here's the secret. You have to own it. Put whatever the fuck makes you feel good on, and then throw your shoulders back and tell the world with your attitude that you are on the inside track of fashion, and they are behind. Be *bold*."

On one occasion, Katherine and I ironically found ourselves at the Ballard Goodwill, which was rumored to have the best clothes (it did live up to the hype!). I held up articles of clothing for approval from the one person with whom I trusted with fashion. To me, these items were either totally hideous or 100 percent genius. The Katherine-factor would tell me which way it tipped. At some point, she stopped me from asking for her opinion and said:

"You're going about this the wrong way. I can't know what's bold for you. You decide what clothes will inspire you to feel bold in how you present yourself to the world."

I still haven't achieved that status—after all, I am a *jeans and hoodie person* at the core of my being—but I have become more adventurous in my journey to outward boldness since that day. Clothes can be an interesting metaphor for vulnerability. Does my lipstick match my shoes? Is every single hair in place? Or are you wearing pajama pants and slippers to Wally World? Because that says a lot too. Being a disheveled mess says, "I don't care enough to put together the minimal effort." I'm sloppy, but just... no. I can't do that.

It's the spectrum in between where you can tiptoe in with personality. Maybe you could wear watermelon earrings or a jelly bracelet in lime green. Maybe you could wear mismatching socks on purpose. Bonus if one of them is a fun pattern like rainbows or kittens. Maybe you're seventeen, and you dress like you are straight out of *Mad Men*. Or maybe you are a forty-something who wants to show some serious skin with a side of curves. Clothes can communicate how you are feeling on the inside.

I would be happy with an entire rack of hoodie after hoodie and twelve pairs of the same comfy jeans in the same color. That feels like home to me. I throw my hair in a sloppy pony bump, and that's my look for the day. On rare occasions, I'll have fancy earrings, curled hair, and a touch of makeup to match my jeans and hoodie. My uniform could feel like armor if I let it. I am self-aware enough to do some damage. Armor or not, these tears still do not quit, regardless of what I am wearing. If only our Instagram grid were our reality. What's on the outside can only be as good as the confidence and honesty on the inside.

While it's a slow process, I am learning that vulnerability is not a weakness. It's a strength. It's brave. Vulnerable people are authentic, courageous, and generous. It takes courage to share your story, your feelings, and your passions with others.

Vulnerability doesn't always happen on a public stage with millions of viewers. It can be sharing something intimate with a loved one, texting a person you haven't spoken to in years, or trying a food you were previously afraid of.

It's my twelve-year-old daughter using a rolling backpack because the weight of the books in a regular one hurt her back. She knows some smart-ass asshole will yell out, "Where's the airport? Goin' on a trip?" Doesn't matter because she's real about what her needs are, a functioning adolescent back—so she's willing to face the scrutiny.

We don't randomly find self-acceptance. We cultivate it through small steps of self-love. Like this. Think of a flaw—maybe that jiggly thigh or the roll on your back—then look in the mirror and tell it, "I love you. You don't need to change. You are enough."

Compliment a stranger. Thank yourself for making a good choice. Forgive someone who doesn't deserve it. Forgive yourself for the things that you can't change. Be divergent in a society of negativity.

Blending in? That's fucking boring. Why be like everyone else when you can be yourself? Be unique. Be different. *Be you.* Who gives a shit if people say you are weird? Good riddance. That's one less opinion to worry about. Embrace it, your weirdness. Your differences are what make you interesting. We need more originality, more creativity, and more authenticity in our lives. Don't be afraid—go out there and be the oddball, beautiful and bold *you* were born to be.

The world waits for you.

CHAPTER 8

The Bitter Grind

Every second of every day of the last eight years led up to this point.

It was my first interview at *the* job, the proverbial pot of gold at the end of the Rainbow of Blah of my previous role. Okay, Rainbow of Blah is a little excessive. It was going nowhere fast with no pay bumps, no growth opportunity, and no excitement in the day-to-day. *This* was my ticket out. Onward and upward.

Admittedly, I applied for the new job on a total whim. It would be worth way more money than I had ever made, and the work managing a multi-provider, the multimillion-dollar practice was more responsibility than I had ever undertaken in my still-fledgling career. The commute would be a little brutal, but I rationalized that having sixty–ninety minutes to myself a day would help me do the other mental planning I needed to do for my ongoing course work for school and household admin tasks (when *was* the last time I bought milk?). Besides, I didn't expect I would even get the interview in the first place.

I walked into the enormous high-rise building in downtown Seattle and rode the elevator up to the thirteenth floor.

If this interview gives me nothing else, I will at least get to enjoy this beautiful view today. The city sprawled out before me as I looked out the window—and then they called my name.

The conversation was unconventional from the jump. In the first question, they asked me my opinion of swearing in the workplace. My face lit up as I explained, "How fucking much I fucking love the word *fuck*." I got a hearty chuckle out of the interviewers. Over the course of the interview, after the people I spoke to told me how much they loved me more times than a clingy high school boyfriend might, a distinct feeling washed over me that maybe, just *maybe*, I did the impossible and nailed it. My suspicions were confirmed as we shook hands upon leaving, and they coyly advised me there was a "strong possibility" I would be the candidate they ultimately hired.

A few days later, I got the email. The one that not only told me I was getting the job but that I was getting the pay. And the corner office. And the benefits. And the commission. More than that, I got the recognition that I was more competent than I imagined with that little email. *Today*, I thought, before I had time to think of a less cliché internal monologue, *is the first day of the rest of my life.*

Before I could begin that new life, I needed to cut ties with my old one. It's important to highlight how much I don't enjoy change, risk, or upheaval of any kind. It's not a secret I love stability, which was why I was even in this position to begin with. Was I making the right choice? *Of course*, I told myself, *you literally did all of this because you wanted a change.*

I was confident enough going in to break the news to my supervisor. I managed to keep my shit together long enough to get it all out, but I crumbled shortly after I finished what I rehearsed. She looked at me kindly (bless her) and shuffled to the back to speak to the doctor. As if I wasn't already embarrassed and teary enough, she called me back into her office a few moments later. She told me the doctor wanted to try and convince me to stay, asking whether there was anything that would persuade me to change my mind.

I'll admit I hesitated. Self-doubt began to creep in at the edges of my brain. *Am I doing the right thing? Did I think this through properly? What if I hate my new job? What if they hate me? Will I do a good job?*

It was too late. My time was up. I knew it, the doctor knew it, my supervisor knew it. My future beckoned, and I wouldn't refuse the call.

* * *

What struck me most upon starting in my new role was the sheer, surprising amount of power I held. Where I was used to feeling like I was being swept along by the current of the whims of others, I suddenly held enough cards in my own young hands to make decisions. But I quickly realized the brutal truth we all learn in our twenties, if not sooner: if it sounds too good to be true, it probably is.

My job was to serve as the liaison between the employees and the doctor—to oversee the team. That sounds great for an outgoing people-person like me, right? Well, turns out there was very little "team" to speak of. The doctor was so temperamental and difficult to communicate with that simply breathing in his general vicinity felt like lighting a match in a room full of diesel fuel. The employees, likely scarred from previous leadership (or a lack thereof), were so disgruntled, disinterested, and utterly checked out that it was practically impossible to get their attention without performing a choreographed burlesque routine. I knew it would take creativity to get these people to gel as a unit. Luckily, I was a mother of two middle school girls and a toddler. The transferrable skills meant I was the Bruce Lee of getting people who wanted to claw each other's throats out to *play fucking nice.*

I scheduled a team meeting which I all but forced the doctor to attend, having prepared a fun *ice breaker* question to get this completely disjointed group of people to bond over something, *anything.* Knowing that these people weren't taking an active interest in each other in the office, I asked each team member to share, "What is the greatest accomplishment that you accomplished before the twelfth grade?"

Lo and behold, the answers were interesting, ranging from competitive sports achievements to academic awards to traveling the world. These people I had been working with for weeks were *not* miserable robots—they were real people with interior lives. My experiment worked. The employees were smiling and laughing with one another, and even the doctor seemed surprisingly engaged.

Maybe I have what it takes to lead this ragtag group of people and this grumpy doctor into greatness. Maybe I was made for this. Sure, the sixty–seventy-hour weeks were getting draining, and the long commute on the light rail started to feel less like I was the main character in my own indie movie, and I found myself disassociating for an hour or more a day. Sure, I have undoubtedly bitten off more than I could chew, but bit by bit, I *was* chewing it.

It wasn't too long before my work wins began to taper off. Remember that *liaison* thing? The main part of the job? Let me break that down for you. I translated the employees' bitching to the doctor in a way he might pretend to listen to. Then, I translated back the doctor's foul-mouthed, name-calling tirades to the employees in a way that wouldn't make them pack up their desks and quit on the spot. My anxiety skyrocketed, and soon, I had panic attacks every day. Every morning, I listened to "Not Afraid" by Eminem with the volume cranked high in my headphones as I walked down the hall to reach the back door to the office. I would stop, shove my shoulders down, and take a huge breath to brace myself for the shit show I was walking into. Then, I would set my stuff down and make coffee *immediately* for the doctor because the part of my job description left out in my offer letter was that I was officially his bitch.

The other aspects of my life were like landmines I couldn't stop stepping on. When I got home at 7:00 or 8:00 p.m., I listened to my older girls tattle on each other and regale the literal fist fights that were happening, bruises and all. Naturally, this was accompanied by extreme guilt; I was letting them stay home alone way too early in life to accommodate this job. What kind of mother lets two middle schoolers fend for themselves? After triaging the argument-du-jour, I headed to the home office to hit the books. I was still working on finishing my bachelor's degree, so it was a rare night I would go to bed before 1:00 a.m. I would then wake at 5:30 or 6:00 a.m. and do it all again.

In the months that followed, my mental state deteriorated faster than I was aware it even could. "Is it abnormal that I have to talk my nerves down every day? I am locked in a battle between ambition and chaos, mom vs. manager, student vs. normal human being," I wrote in my diary. The curmudgeonly doctor who owned my ass was cutting benefits left and right, and one of the ones I personally depended on, tuition reimbursement, was most likely on the line. I was also the unfortunate one tasked with the impossible job of looking hardworking employees in the eye and telling them their compensation was reduced. I tried to convince myself that I was high up enough within the practice to be immune to the cuts, but the truth is, I wasn't.

So I stressed and stressed and stressed. I worried about work, my babies, my rapidly increasing weight, and its impact on my overall health. I stressed about my lack of sleep, which apparently is a great way to lose even more sleep. I worried about whether I was a good example to the girls and whether I was failing them as a mother. I agonized over the other employees at the practice and whether they were happy. Then there were my stupid fucking grades. The entire experience so completely broke me. What did I have to show for it? A family in shambles? Barely passable assignments? The glamorous title of Personal Barista for the World's Worst Boss? I was drowning in a hell of my own creation.

This was the job I dreamed of my whole life, the job that would show me my value. This title and position were supposed to mean I was worth something. It would mean I was big enough to be recognized. It was all a sham.

After a year of pushing myself to the brink of full *Girl, Interrupted* insanity, my saving grace came in the form of a tantalizing offer from another practice. The pay was comparable, the work was similar, and I took it before I could change my mind. I was free, but I still felt hollow. Although I was grateful the experience was over, worries about the time I'd wasted ate away at me. Spoiler alert: the next job was much the same. Aside from a shorter commute and fewer life-eating hours spent at the new practice, my new boss was a new cranky doctor, and there were new frustrated employees to manage.

It was only years later I realized the thing I imagined was going to give me a sense of self-worth turned out to be a more fucked up red herring than seen on any rerun of *Scooby-Doo*. The thing that helped me unlock that sense of my own innate value was *letting it all go*. That year of my life, consumed by crappy doctors, angry subordinates, and an utter lack of life outside of work, dissolved all the expectations of what success was and what it would look like when *I made it*. The actual goalpost, it turns out, is always moving. Even when I landed *the dream job*, I still grappled with insecurities and how much more I could have been doing. When I left that job, it was no time at all before I had an entirely new set of arbitrary metrics against which I measured my own success. I would rinse and repeat a few more times before the lesson stuck.

It turns out I was a success already during that time. My girls still love me, I finished the degree and graduated Magna Cum Laude, and by finding out that I did not dream of making coffee for irritable MD after irritable M for the rest of my life, I was able to figure out what I *did* want (more on that later).

And hey, I still make a mean cup of coffee.

CHAPTER 9

A Drop Too Much

Sometimes when you lose big time, you hit the jackpot of winning yourself back. Rock bottom is where we learn *we are more* than the pain. *We are more* than the heartbreak. *We are more* than our mistakes, poor choices, or even who let us down.

Everyone will come to a time in life where they will be alone, defeated, and broken all at once. It is inevitable because you cannot go through life without experiencing loss (and I'm not talking only about someone dying). Unfortunately for me, I had to learn this life lesson the hard way.

In the fall of 2018, my life spiraled. I was about to be forty years old, unemployed, and failing in every aspect of my life.

One fine Friday, I showed up to my clusterfuck of a workplace and was called into the manager's office. I took a deep breath and tried to roll my shoulders back a bit. I knew. I knew what was going to happen because of what had happened the day before.

Earlier in the week, I checked the paper schedule in the assistants' station, and it said I had Thursday off. But bright and early Thursday morning, I got a call from my manager, Lydia, who sighed in annoyance before talking.

"Riah, why aren't you here?"

I answered, super confused. "... Because I'm off?"

"No, you most definitely are *not* off, and now we are short-handed."

I offered to head in right away, but she told me not to bother.

An angry and frustrated pit formed in my stomach. This type of mix-up was not new. Management had a habit of switching the schedule at the last minute and not telling me. Then, even though I was diligent in keeping track of which days I was supposed to work, it was somehow my fault when I arrived late or not at all. What's the point of even putting up a schedule two weeks in advance if you're going to change it constantly? After our phone call, I was distinctly awake. I laid in bed that night stewing at the injustice and the guilt.

The next day I showed up early. I was showered, in fresh scrubs with a dusting of light makeup on my face. I needed whatever armor I could cling to for the ass-chewing that was to ensue.

I was making myself scarce in the X-ray closet when Lydia came in. I noticed she was wearing scrubs. My heart sunk. She only wore scrubs if she needed to replace someone for the day on the clinical team. This situation was not going to end well for me, but I was still in denial. She called me back to the doctor's office.

She got right to the point. "This isn't working. Riah, you're fired. Effective immediately."

I swallowed hard, and the tears stung my eyes. I tried to fight them back. Lydia corralled me to the lunchroom and took my keys after I cleared out my locker. The pace she was pushing me out of the office was urgent even though I gave her no reason for aggression.

"Don't worry," I assured her. "I'm not going to say anything or make a fuss." I tried to hurry. I could tell she was rushing me, and I didn't want to hang out and make small talk. "I am going to have to apply for unemployment," I told her, and she bobbed her head affirmatively.

"Yep, no problem. You have to go now," Lydia said. She seemed sincere, and the belief I would have unemployment benefits gave me comfort. I would soon find out she and the doctors later compiled a whole bullshit case against me to deny my unemployment for *grievous misconduct*, a.k.a they kept records saying I was late on days I was not. When I learned the insult of termination had turned to an injury of unemployment denial, I consulted a lawyer to see if I could fight it. Embarrassingly, she said my previous employers had collected significant evidence against me, and I had nothing to prove to the contrary. They knew they were going to let me go and made preparations to do so. I was caught with my pants down.

Being fired was, in some ways, a blessing. The job was pure toxicity. The leadership and my coworkers made me miserable and treated me like absolute shit. Often, I would come around a corner, and my teammates would instantly stop talking at look up guiltily at me. The cliques were strong, and I did not belong. Most days after my shift, I sobbed in my car in the empty parking lot. For the first time in my adulthood, I questioned my value as an employee and, in earnest, as a person. I was continually torn down and treated condescendingly.

My alcohol consumption ramped up because of this. I was under a ton of pressure and trapped in misery. After my shift, or after I finished crying, I would frequently stop at Applebee's and head straight to the bar. I would sit and sip my sorrow down until it was time to go. It was always too many drinks. I would often take a nap in my car in the parking lot to make sure I was safe to drive. Once I got fired, the drinking amped up. I had already been drinking heavily, then it kicked into hyperdrive, including multiple times I drove home drunk.

I had only stayed at the job solely to gain the clinical experience for an application to a prestigious post-graduate program at Seattle University I had my eye on. I was dead set on making it into the program. Even though I should have quit the shitty job a million times over, I would imagine graduating from SU and would stay. Getting fired was humiliating, but most of all, it meant I would not have the required clinical experience to get into Seattle University. My prospects of getting another clinical job with a recent termination under my belt were impossible.

Temptation taunted me and dangled the carrot of giving up on my dreams, but I didn't want to let myself down.

Maybe I could make this work after all. I wanted to prove everyone wrong who said I wouldn't amount to much in life. I put one foot in front of the other and went through the motions, even though I was dead inside. I figured I would try to focus on the Anatomy and Physiology class kicking my butt. I hoped the extra free time would give me the chance I needed to raise my grade. I was trying *so hard* to memorize everything, but the stress of home and kids and losing my job... everything was too much.

It came crashing down. All it had taken to get to that place in my career, to come right to the edge of reaching my dream, all the education, work sacrifices, family sacrifices, financial sacrifices, and *poof*—everything was gone. I told myself it would all work out, but I didn't believe myself. I was in a dark hole, I was scrambling, and I couldn't see a way out.

Every day was a battle, and I was losing more and more of myself. My counselor at the time, Bonnie, would correct me any time I said I was unemployed. "Riah, you have two clients you're helping on the side. In my opinion, you are 'self-employed.'"

Self-employed or not, things were not well. Beer felt like the only thing keeping me from going over the edge. I had horrible nightmares and night terrors. I often woke up screaming or crying. If I didn't wake myself, my husband would have to wake me up because otherwise, it wouldn't stop. I began drinking myself to sleep. A six-pack of Blue Moon with a side of OJ to add a citrusy flavor. I could (and usually did) polish off all six. I kept the six-pack on my side of the bed and would sip them as I wound down for the evening. It was the only way I could keep the dream monsters away. Otherwise, I would lie awake for hours, and then I was tortured in my sleep.

Then there was also the complicated dynamic at home. Despite repeatedly asking, it was difficult getting family members to help with my dad's caregiving. The tension between my husband and I was palpable with all that was going on. Looking back, I see I was using alcohol to self-medicate and to numb what I couldn't control. It only made things worse.

I kept going to therapy, and Bonnie would ask me about the drinking. I admitted I drank but always lied about how much. Looking back, I see how pointless lying to a counselor was, but I thought I was retaining a shred of dignity at the time. What pointless dignity.

Ultimately all this failure culminated in dropping the Anatomy and Physiology class I was taking because my brain couldn't... science. Losing the clinical experience, followed by the failed attempt to pass the final class I also needed for my application, meant my dream of getting into the program at Seattle University was truly dead. My soul felt dead too. *What the fuck am I supposed to do with my life now?* My professional goals were in shambles. I was failing as a wife, a mother, and a daughter. I was failing myself and losing myself in the process. I was spinning out of control.

Even though I was drinking more than ever, I did sincerely try to hold it together. I wanted my kids to have a regular mom and dad. I wanted them to see that no matter how bad things seem now, they will eventually get better. I wanted them to know I was fighting for a better life, and I wasn't going to fall apart. But the edges were frayed, and they saw anyway.

One night, I took my then fifteen-year-old and my seven-year-old to dinner. I tried not to, but I drank too much. I thought I would be okay, but I was past okay. Sloppy and slurring my words, I planned to drive them the fifteen-minute ride home. Instead, my middle daughter had to literally pry the keys from my fingers and drive us home. She had no experience driving, no permit, no license, and we lived on a highway. When we got home, she shifted the car into park and ushered my youngest inside. I sat for a bit in the driveway. I sank into the passenger side seat and let the guilt wash over my drunk-ass self. I was the stupidest fuck. I experienced waves of shame pummeling me over and over again, and I deserved it. I put my kids at risk, and for what? A few moments to numb the pain?

The next day, I apologized profusely to both my girls and promised it would never happen again. I kept that promise but also kept my solid six by the bed to help me sleep. At least I wasn't driving, right?

Like most of us, I had previously seen my life in terms of miles remaining until the end. The plan was simple: get good grades in school, become a nurse practitioner, make lots of money, and do something to make this world a better place. I worked for an entire decade to apply to an advanced nursing program I was passionate about. I should have been celebrating a successful acceptance into the program. Instead, failure ripped the rug out from underneath me. This turmoil caused a massive identity crisis, and I didn't cope at all. I let my family down financially, professionally, and personally. My fortieth birthday passed with little fanfare. What was there to celebrate?

I started half-heartedly looking for a new job, but nothing spurred me to action. Indeed.com taunted me with job after job that I was over or underqualified for. I cried while scrolling. Though we desperately needed the money, I lived in fear of applying. I couldn't stomach more rejection. Additionally, without the program at Seattle U, my resume and healthcare experience made no sense. If I wasn't going to pursue healthcare anymore, what was the point of my twenty years of experience in the field? More importantly, what if the people interviewing me asked me why my last employer fired me? What would I say then?

My anxiety was paralyzing, compounded by my repeated self-damnation. I did this to myself. Me. I also did this to my family, who needed me to contribute financially. They were suffering because of what a loser I was. I could blame it all on the toxicity of the workplace (which was 100 percent true), but I shared responsibility. I showed up late to the office many times. My tardiness was often justified, but none of it mattered now.

I finally sucked it up and began applying to anything I was qualified for. I would take any honest work at this point, but not one place I applied for called back. The sun was setting on my professional life too early, and I didn't know how to stop it.

I kept working (poorly but consistently) for my friends, doing administrative work for them for a few hours once a week. They didn't say anything, but I could see they felt sorry for me and kept me on to keep me from falling off the edge. I decided to legitimize my work and get a business license because I no longer had any other income coming in. I didn't consider myself *in business*, but my sister encouraged me to pick a name, get a logo, and a website.

"What for? Literally, like, what the fuck for? I am not in business—I don't want to get in trouble with the IRS for evading taxes."

"Dude, you *are* in business. Do this. Embrace this," my sister encouraged me.

I snorted, "If you think this 'business' should have a name, be my guest."

Then and there, Admin Prestige was born.

Rock bottom is not a pretty place, but it can be the birthplace of beautiful things. Recognize this period of your life, this embarrassing, agonizing time, is the *foundation* on which your success rests. *You can't win if you don't defeat.* You are not your mistakes or your shame. You are more than the pain. You can still succeed. Cling to that. I know you can.

I had to come to grips with the absolute fucking destruction I was causing for myself and those around me. Continuing down the path I was on was no longer an option. I was watching my life happen around me, but I was numb to all of it. I was hurting myself. I was hurting my loved ones. I could have hurt someone else. Something had to give, and I decided to make a change, crawl out of the hole I dug myself, and drag the unwilling part of me along for the ride.

I don't remember the exact day I stopped drinking, except it was on or around my forty-first birthday. The

Blue Moon six-pack habit had become so ingrained I wondered if it would even be physically possible to stop. I had to give myself a reality check that I may have given myself an addiction. So somewhere in the vicinity of my birthday, I didn't stop at the gas station on the way home to buy beer, which was my daily habit. I cruised past it and just kept driving until I made it home. I went to bed early that night. The sleep demons were waiting, but it wasn't as bad as I remembered. The next morning, I researched AA meetings and found one far enough from where we lived that I wouldn't run into anyone I knew.

I walked in and gingerly took a seat. I crouched my tall frame down in shame and made myself small. Maybe no one would see me. Not so lucky.

The chairperson walked straight up to me, "Hi there. I'm Joan. You're new here, aren't you?"

I nodded in response but didn't speak. It was as if talking in this room would make what I was doing a reality. I wasn't even sure if I belonged here.

We took turns speaking. One man celebrated ten years of sobriety; another woman had fallen off the wagon the day before after six years of being alcohol-free. She cried into soaked tissues until someone passed her more. Then it was my turn.

I didn't want to admit I was an alcoholic because, in truth, I didn't know if I was. I knew I had a problem but wasn't sure what that meant for me.

I cleared my throat. "Hi. I'm Riah."

"Hi Riah," everyone chimed.

"This is my second day without drinking."

Joan looked over at me and whispered, "You're in the right place." That was kind of her, but in my heart, I wasn't so sure.

"I've been drinking every day for the last few years, and I'm finally ready to start living again. I'm so sick of being sad. I'm tired of being tired of my life." Knowing nods around the room.

The rest of the hour passed in a daze. Afterward, the group leader passed around scraps of paper and a basket for people to put their phone numbers on them for me. I didn't linger. They were beautiful humans, and I could see why this was the best path for many, but AA was not for me. I got myself into this mess, and I was going to find my way out. I needed to reconnect with my family, come clean with my counselor, and get the meaningful support I needed desperately.

A week after I quit drinking, I admitted everything to my counselor. I told her I had been downplaying things for a long time.

"You're not a great liar, Riah. I already knew. I was waiting for you to admit it to yourself." Sneaky one, Bonnie.

I woke up on day three with a headache but a sense of accomplishment. I turned over to my husband and said, "I am done drinking."

He blinked, trying to wake up, and looked straight at me. "Really?"

"Really."

In the days following, I announced my tally of days of sobriety to my loved ones every morning. I downloaded an app that showed me (to the hour) how long I had been alcohol-free and how much money I saved by not buying my usual supply.

"Good morning, honey," I would tell my eldest daughter, Angie. "It's been nine days since I drank."

She'd reach over and give me a heartfelt high-five. "Good job, Momma. I'm proud of you."

With alcohol slowly coming under control, another area that I could no longer ignore was being an entrepreneur. Unwittingly or not, I had to take ownership of the fact that I was now a business owner. Despite my pitiful attempts to thwart it, business was starting to take off. I needed to focus on reconciliation and ownership of my shit.

Bottom line: maybe your life *is* a shit show, but recovery *in all its forms* is a major win. Recognition of personal shit is a win. Fighting for oneself is a win. Let's take a moment to see where we are destructive to our own badassery and how can we find at least one fucking win in that bag of crap.

Success doesn't need to look gorgeous or wrapped with a beautiful bow. You are successful if you choose four beers instead of six. Success can be drinking yourself sloppy at home instead of a bar where you risk choosing to drive drunk. It likely isn't the best choice overall, but it is better than the alternative. There might be shame in these successes, but they are still valid wins. Take the win.

Listen, grand achievement might not start out as a fantastical portrait. We are a game of shit-show-connect-the-dots. Draw one little line from one little dot of success to the next little dot of success, and eventually, we make up the greater picture of something wonderful. Please don't minimize the accomplishments in your lows. They are just as—nay, *more*—important than the successes in your highs. It's just harder to see them.

Just because to someone else, they may look like failures; you know the truth. You know you made a *less sucky* choice over a *suckier* choice. I see you—hell, *I see me*. I'm so proud of us.

CHAPTER 10

Crash into Me

Do you ever find yourself feeling frustrated with your life because nothing is going the way it's supposed to?

Most of the time, it feels like my life is cruising along, doing its own thing, and I'm riding bitch. Life takes unexpected twists and turns that lead us in new directions. Good or bad, we must learn to navigate them without completely getting lost. Life's GPS is permanently rerouting, and we have to master the art of following along.

February 8, 2020, I was ignoring any form of GPS.

It was raining, and I was late. *Damn it all.* There was traffic for miles on the 405. I knew I shouldn't, but I threw that left-hand blinker on and inched my way over to the HOV lane. The traffic in that lane was still heavy, still slow, but at least at a steady pace. Then stop, go, stop, go. It was a dance of impatient drivers, and I was tangoing right along with them. Traffic finally picked up, and we were at sixty mph for five minutes.

Then it happened. My purse started to dump over on the passenger seat, and instinctively, I threw my right arm out to stop it. Any woman who has had to put back together the abyss of a tipped-over purse knows the urgency of that thrown-out arm. The bigger problem is that in preventing the chaos of an overturned purse, I turned my head away from the road for a split fucking second.

I barely remember what happened next. I glanced back up through the windshield and saw a green 4Runner in front of me now stopped. I slammed on my brakes, but I *knew* I was about to slam into that car, ram myself all the way to the front, and my life was about to change.

My arms cranked left.

There was an impact, but I remember nothing of it. Disoriented, I slowly surveyed my surroundings. I saw the large, white airbag deflated. It was still smoking and burning a hole in my pants. The contents of my purse were scattered. Well, so much for that. The crash flung my cell phone to the far corner of the passenger side floor. I checked my body. No blood I could see, but my left wrist looked contorted into a freakish shape. My brain couldn't comprehend the way that it looked. I couldn't hold my left arm up. I leaned my head back in the seat and closed my eyes for a second. So. Much. Pain. And fear. And shame. I knew better.

A man and a woman from the car behind me rushed to the driver's side window. "Are you okay?" the woman asked.

I bleakly lifted my left wrist and shook my head. No, definitely not. "Please call my husband."

I gave them the number, but he didn't answer. I had them call my daughter. No answer. Then my sister. No response. The ambulance arrived, and I sobbed while riding along with the EMT in the back while the sirens rang out. I had him call all of them three more times, but nothing.

Eventually, someone got ahold of my daughter, who then, in turn, was finally able to reach my husband, who was farther away. My daughter, Angelica, raced to the hospital and was the first to be with me. She told me she had passed my car on the side of the freeway. She had hit the traffic, and when she saw it was my car, she sobbed. She imagined its mangled shell was only a clue as to how broken I would be.

I arrived at the hospital, and immediately the staff ushered me into a room. Angie arrived not too much longer after me. It turned out I had a broken wrist (duh), and because I am an overachiever, I broke the top of my radius off and required a plate to put it all together again. The doctors almost missed that I had a horrific clavicle fracture because they were so worried about my wrist. I kept asking, "Can I have a pillow or something to prop up my arm?" Just the weight of holding it up was killing me.

Finally, a doctor took note of my repeated request, "Where's the upper body CT scan?" His face contorted in disgust when the nurses told him they had only taken X-rays of my wrist. Back to radiology I went.

Angie went with me to the X-ray department. She leaned over when they were getting me situated back in the ER. She whispered, "I'm not supposed to tell you yet, but your collarbone is *fucked.*" Five gold stars for me because that massive break in my left collarbone also required a surgical plate to put me back together again. Just call me Humpty Dumpty.

Over the next month, surgeries and more pain ensued. All this happened on the eve of the pandemic. The weirdness and grief of that global catastrophe only made my recovery more complex. During the healing process, my collarbone never felt right. I continued to have severe pain that took the wind out of me for weeks.

Throughout this time, my husband was my rock. He drove me to appointments that he wasn't allowed into due to protocols. He bought me heat packs and cold packs. He picked up medications and did anything I asked him to. I began to lean on the comfort of having my partner be present for me.

I had never experienced a period of physical limitation like this, and for once, I had no choice but to ask for help.

Not at full capacity yet, and against the wishes of everyone who loved me, I wanted to stay independent where I could. Recovery be damned, I threw myself back into work almost immediately. I needed to *do* something to fix all of this. I was not confident that time or healing would improve things. I was careful not to physically compromise myself, but I couldn't just lay in bed and feel incessant pain.

But at every orthopedic follow-up, the doctor said everything looked stable. Over time, I felt like the pain of healing was not easing up and sensed something was off. After eight weeks of telling the surgeon that something felt so painful and seriously wrong, we did yet another check-up X-ray. This one was different than the rest.

All of the screws in my plate had come out, and the puzzle piece of a clavicle was floating free. Surgery. Again. But this time, we had to petition for an emergency procedure: no surgery center, only an in-hospital operating room due to the COVID-19 pandemic.

Several days later, my husband, daughter, and I showed up at the hospital the morning of the surgery. We were met at the door by scowling nurses. "Only the patient can go in," they said.

I protested, "I'm having surgery! Can't I have my family with me? It's just two of them!"

The nurses were adamant, and I turned to my husband with so much pain. Everything hurt—body, mind, soul. I was scared and wanted my husband with me, but I put on a brave face, as was expected of me. Just when I was learning to accept the love and help from others, I was going to have to face this alone.

He gently kissed my head and whispered, "You'll be okay, and I'll be waiting outside in the car the whole time."

I turned on my heel and walked through the thick plastic tarps hanging down to secure off sections of the hospital. Tears streamed down my face as I made my way to surgery, step-by-hesitant-step. I wasn't afraid of the surgery itself. I was scared it wouldn't work. I feared the constant pain that reminded me every day of my stupid, stupid decision to catch my purse while driving inappropriately in the HOV lane in traffic. It reminded me I am so stubborn sometimes it takes a cement wall—or a green 4Runner—to stop me.

In later months, I tried to work through the transformational healing I needed to move forward. I was traumatized physically and emotionally. The doctors worked on healing my body, but my heart was a different story. I tried many types of healing—Theta healing, Reiki, Inner Child work, prayer, and Core Wound Healing. I struggled to find a way to move past the pain. I was confused why all this had happened.

I was embarrassed I had caused a car accident for a stupid reason. I felt exposed and profoundly sad. I didn't know how to break the habit of moving through life too fast and doing everything independently. All this started because I run myself ragged in life—a mistaken belief that a successful life is a busy one. I was running metaphorical red lights right and left. I held firmly to the belief that I had to do it alone.

There are so many lies I believed about surrendering for so long. One day, I sat down and put my pen to paper (well, Apple pencil to iPad, but you get what I'm saying.) I listed all the reasons why surrendering to the Universe was a horrible idea. These were my limiting beliefs:

Surrender is weakness.

No one can save me.

I am the only person I can count on.

I don't have the luxury of falling apart. If I fall apart, I will die because I will be exposed and unprotected.

No one cares if I am in pain. I have to hide my pain because it makes people uncomfortable.

I can't let go. I'm too scared. If I let go, there will be nothing left of me.

I cannot trust.

Trusting leads to heartache, betrayal, and a bleeding soul.

I cannot surrender.

I knew that addressing these limiting beliefs and the scars on my heart would help me in the journey to heal my body too. My more logical brain knew none of these things were true, but they embossed themselves on my heart.

Sleep often escaped me in those weeks. I would lay in a position that wouldn't hurt for a while, and then my body would ache, and I would gingerly flip. All the time, my anxious mind never quit. Why am I so dumb? What if I hadn't done that? Will my heart ever stop aching? What the fuck am I going to do with this business that is now in full swing?

Rarely, late in the night or early in the morning, I would fall asleep deeply. My body was profoundly tired—physically, emotionally, spiritually—and would mercifully give out.

After one such night, I woke up to words writing themselves in my head. I could see the letters and almost hear the narration. There was an urgency to get them out before they disappeared. I kept a journal close to my bed and leaned over to pour this message out onto the page. I scribbled the words and tried to make sense of it all. I prayed and meditated… and then I wrote some more.

My answers to prayer often come in the form of letters back to me, and this was no exception. As my hand moved across the page, I could hear the Universe speaking to me. The words echoed softly in my ears.

"My chosen child,

Did you know that angels are real? They are my protectors and warriors, and I have a fuck-ton of them flocked around you at all times. Your life was saved because I am not ready for you to come back to me yet. You have work to do and lives to touch.

You are going to have to use your voice, and you will have to ask for help. When you feel the most fear, the most alone... close your eyes. Gently place your hand over your heart. Yes, right on that scar leftover from that life-altering day. Now breathe. Be still.

Do you feel it? The gentle brush of wings around you? Riah, your Earthly loved ones may be far away at times, but we are right here. It is safe to ask me for help. It is safe to speak about your needs. I will listen. I will meet and exceed them. I will never leave you.

You are not an inconvenience to me. I long to hear your voice. Tell me your stories. Start from the beginning, and don't stop until you've been genuinely filled to the brim with my love and attention.

I will not leave you alone. Think of these angels as your badass heavenly secret service, ready to take a bullet on your behalf. You are special to me, and as any parent should, I will fight for you as you have never seen before. Speak to me, my love. I'm listening.

Your Divine Dad"

My heart woke up. This letter from God catalyzed my healing and dispelled the limiting beliefs I had stubbornly held onto for far too long. He was right: I could ask for help. I'd have to if I ever wanted to heal. People like my loyal husband and loving daughters did care I was in pain and responded to help me heal.

I could rest easy knowing if my "Earthly loved ones" were unreachable, I could call upon my winged bodyguards and my Divine Dad to support me, to catch me when I let go. I could also accept the crash as a gift because I was running myself ragged before it happened. It literally stopped me.

At the time, there was no direction or clarity on why I was doing things the way I was in my business or personal life. Some people like to let life go by quickly. Maybe they do this because it is easier than slowing down and experiencing their lives. Other people slow down so much that they don't even seem to be living at all. I have passed through both phases in my life but have always leaned into the fast lane more than the alternative.

Maybe some people need physical trauma or emotional difficulty to realize how vital slowing down can be. If you don't savor the little things, life can sneak up on you and stop you instead. These days I tell myself, "Don't rush through it. Slow down, take a deep breath. Just let life happen around you and cherish everything." I still move too fast often in my business. Who the fuck knows where I think I'm headed? The reminder to slow the hell down is only one glance down at the bumpy scar on my shoulder blade away.

Mistakes will happen. Heartbreak will happen. Failure will happen. We need help. We need to trust and let people in. If we trust in nothing, we will be out in the cold, weathering the elements while we wait for it to get better. On our own, surrendering is a very difficult process. Success doesn't happen by accident, and it very rarely happens alone. We need to be able to trust something or someone in order to move into a more actualized self. You need to surrender to something you believe is unshakable.

For me, that's God/Universe/Higher Power. Fuck, even the highest version of yourself works! For others, it might be science, or it might be the void of nothing. But there must be trust in something outside of humans who, even at their best, are totally fallible.

How can you start the trusting process? What are your limiting beliefs, and who are the people in your life who might be able to help you overcome them? Then, consider what spiritual entity you might believe in. Write it all down. Bust out your smartphone notes app. Type like a mofo.

Don't speed through life, and don't do it by yourself all the time. You deserve to have someone in your passenger seat. Let them hold your purse before it tips over. Two sets of eyes are better than one, and together, you just might avoid the crash.

CHAPTER 11

In the Middle

Sometimes we focus so much on what's happening outside that we forget to appreciate what's happening inside. Imagine if you only looked at the outside of the cup, not knowing it contains something delicious to drink. You would never get to taste what you are searching for because you are basing everything on looks alone. The same happens when we are searching for the highs in life or wallowing in the lows.

We often have long stretches of time that might be called *blah* because they seem to drag on, and we aren't actively working on something to better ourselves or advance in some way. In those stretches of time, moments live where we learn to cope, love, and be kinder to ourselves. These times we often forget to appreciate the beauty of the common parts of our life.

For example, when you are in the middle of a good book or story, do you not enjoy it? I think that is why movies have so many twists and turns. Because we get bored easily with the monotony of life, writers spice things up by adding more action to keep our attention. What if we just appreciate the natural twists and turns instead of forcing them? What if time could slow enough or stand still enough that we aren't hung up on the past or anxious about the future. You are just completely in the moment feeling all the sensations that come with it.

These thoughts came to me when I was recently going through years of photos on my computer. I flipped through one after another, and the tears misted up in my eyes. I saw photos of my oldest daughters in their adorable little girl phases and watched as they changed into their awkward years of middle school. These were some of my favorites because these photos showed them experimenting with makeup, parting their hair *way* too far to the side, and smiling with the hidden sadness that can often sit inside a preteen's heart.

It took me right back to these moments in my life, preteen or otherwise, when I thought what I was doing didn't make a difference or nothing special was happening. These are the parts of life where we attempt to survive or simply exist as best as we can. But I realized we can be in the middle of *nothing* and still be successful. Doing our best now is enough.

Success doesn't have to be loud to exist. It does not require pomp and circumstance. No balloons or exorbitant celebrations are required. What matters is how we grow in the ordinary parts of life when there aren't any fireworks to commemorate it. There can be triumph in a whisper. Victory can be an experience so painful that it burns—but it teaches us the most valuable lesson.

An example for me is the forming of positive habits. I forget things all the time. My lousy memory has cost me quality time, stress, actual money, so many debit cards, and I can't even count how many sets of keys. Setting a system into place and then watching it work because I can routinely find what I am looking for feels amazing.

These aren't participation ribbons we are talking about here. Regular life may be less exciting than the more momentous parts, but it deserves to be acknowledged all the same. If we let ourselves stop spinning long enough to learn from these moments of achievement, maybe we can move forward with our heads held a little higher. That's where our real strength and growth happens, anyway. We may stumble in the process, but in the end, we are better for it.

I'm a middle child. It's part of my everyday life and how things have always shaken out in the pecking order of my nuclear family. Growing up, I always promised myself that I would never have three children because uneven numbers equal someone's getting passed over. The oldest gets everything new, goes through all the milestones first, and gets a lot of attention for being special and, well... first.

Then everything the baby does is perfect. She's a cherub of goodness. It feels as if she can do no wrong.

In my family, my youngest sister almost died at birth, so, on top of being the baby, she was the *miracle baby*. People came to the house to ooh and ahh over her, and they only noticed me long enough to say, "Aren't you excited about being a big sister?" I was shy to begin with, so it wasn't too hard to slip further into the shadows after her birth. For most of my life (and in truth, sometimes still), I felt sandwiched between the different types of attention my sisters needed. I tried to forge my way with independence because I felt unseen. I often feel that if my family can't see that I need it, then it is just easier to provide it for myself.

Middle children often feel unnoticed and struggle to find a sense of identity, much like how we feel in the middle of our lives. It's during these times we might wear bright colors to feel seen or start writing to find our voice. The middle of life can be a combination of many emotions, and not just bad or good. It takes patience and acceptance to be in the middle because we often feel like we're never enough. There's this idea if we work harder, do more, and try harder, then maybe we'll finally earn a sense of acknowledgment. "If only I could..." we lament.

In February 2001, the blue-eyed bub that was supposed to be my last child made her appearance in this world. She quickly grew from a bald baby who slept like a champ into a mop of curls and big emotions. Marisol was an ocean of sweetness packed in a little body. She called very little attention to herself. She smiled often and wanted desperately to be just like her big sister.

My husband and I were solidly in the middle years: stressed about money, buying our first home in preparation for giving the girls a better school district, taking life's punches, and trying to keep a brave face. We got a lot wrong, and one of those things was mistaking Marisol's lack of demands for a lack of need for attention. I tried to love her as much as I tried to protect her from the harsh realities of school and unkind kids. But I was not always there when she needed me, and she was there, also caught *in the middle*—so preciously important but not showered enough with the attention she deserved and needed.

When we told her she was going to be a big sister at eight years old, she bawled.

"Why would you do that?" she yelled as we sat in a BBQ restaurant with a tiny, printed ultrasound on the table between us. I can only imagine she thought we would forget her altogether, lost in a crowd of three children. Little did she know the tiny human on that ultrasound would end up being a huge source of joy and recognition for her later in life. She and her younger sister are inseparable despite the eight years between them. Becoming a big sister lit her up, and it feels so good to watch her now be idolized by our youngest for the amazing person that she is.

Almost every year in the last decade, on August 12th, I text Marisol a meme that depicts a cartoon of an irritated kid with his arms crossed. It reads, "Happy Middle Child's Day! Oh, you didn't notice it's Middle Child's Day? Don't worry, no one ever does." It's marked as extra ironic because some years, I forget. Is she invalid when I forget? Hardly. Should I do better? One hundred percent.

I recently came across an 8mm recording. A tiny cassette that snapped into an ancient video recorder. As the picture started, I saw that it was my husband filming the girls playing in the living room of our old house. Angie looked about four, and Marisol had to have been only two at the time. She was running around in only her diaper.

There was nothing significant about this moment. He was just filming daily life, talking to the girls and asking them questions. They were lightly pushing each other, then racing from one side of the room to the other. The high-pitched baby voices mixed with hyper giggles tickled my ears and warmed my heart.

My eldest, Angie, left the camera's view, and hubby zoomed in on Solly. Marisol was just twirling around and playing by herself. He hid the camera under the blanket because he knew her curiosity about the camera would stop the beauty in action he was capturing. He chuckled, and she looked over in his direction. She stopped abruptly, zeroed in on the camera, and made a beeline for it, declaring, "I shee! I shee!" This was baby talk for "I want to see!" Marisol didn't understand. As soon as she stepped behind the camera, the magic would be over, and there would be nothing left to see. *She* was the magic.

Guys, *we* are what there is to see. Even underappreciated or inadequately loved, we are worthy of being seen.

I wonder what Marisol's experience would have been like if my husband and I had spent a little more time honoring the kid she was in her early years instead of just pushing through for the sake of our own sanity. If I had forced us to slow down and recognize what mattered, maybe she would have felt less invisible.

While she was home for the holidays in 2021, I let Marisol read through the first run of this chapter.

"It's nice, Mom… but where's the conflict?"

She meant it both from the point of view of a storyteller herself and also as a pragmatic daughter. We do have a long history with a shit ton of conflict, that child and me. I used to think it was because we are so similar, but after the conversations that followed this one, I don't think that anymore.

"Fine, you're right. I should share more about how we've struggled over the years. Can I interview you?" I said.

She agreed, and I began prepping. I was nervous and bracing myself because I knew there were going to be things that would be hard to hear. I wasn't asking soft questions. This book is about owning our shit and still making it out the other side with our soul intact after all. The questions were direct, beyond what I'm normally comfortable with.

I printed the list of questions and let her read them so she wouldn't feel ambushed. After reviewing the questions, suddenly she had no interest in providing feedback. I asked her, "So what's the scoop? You just don't want to do the interview anymore?"

"I'd rather not. Just write whatever you want."

Well, shit. That was not the point. Now I worried I would add the conflict to this chapter, and it would be all lopsided with solely my perspective. Here I was trying to be fair and trying to listen.

I called her into my office to talk about it later that day. I asked her why she had a change of heart, and she took a controlled breath and then calmly unloaded a whole can of worms. She shared her take on the life I had given her so far, some good sprinkled with a fair share of trauma and sadness mixed in.

She said she felt like we had never parented her, that my husband and I had failed to provide the safety net she needed. She felt ignored and that she had to take care of herself. She also explained she doesn't like talking to me about these things because I'm too emotional, making her feel like I make everything about me. A jolt went through my body when she said that. I realized then we really aren't similar at all, and it broke my heart.

Her words cut deep, and I longed to change her mind, make her see somehow what had been happening behind the scenes. I bit my tongue with the defensive words that want so badly to have a voice. Like most mothers, I know I have so many shortcomings, but I really had tried. I felt a piece of my soul die listening to her explain her perspective of how I fell short. Nothing she said was false. I tried so hard to just listen, for once, to just *pay attention to her.*

Tears betrayed me and slipped onto my right cheek as I sucked in the sadness. I love this kid so much. As a young mother, I had promised I would always love my babies in the way I needed. I would be a provider, a comfort, and a refuge. I had failed.

I cried every day for two weeks after that talk. I woke with body aches from the grief that consumed me. I kept replaying the words, and I felt her pain. I wanted a do-over.

I was desperate to go back and hold the smaller version of her when she felt alone. I imagined diffusing one of our arguments in the car when she was a teenager, taking a breath to center myself, and then telling her she was loved and never a burden to me.

I imagined slipping a note to the past version of me that *Parent Night for Young Actors* is *a big deal. She will tell you it's not important because she thinks you won't care, but when you don't show up, it will scar her. Just go, Riah. Show up.*

Just because Marisol didn't express it all the time didn't mean she didn't need her mom. I will have to grow to accept that I can't undo or redo anything that happened in the past. I can only hope my apologies count for something and be present now.

As I take inventory of this ride of motherhood I've been on, I see how much I realize I didn't show up for myself either. In those periods of time when my girls were little, there are whole years that I barely remember. I look at pictures of myself from those years and see the younger face, the thinner profile, but then I look in my eyes. Those eyes say, "I am so tired. I'm barely hanging on here." I was trying (and failing) to do so many things at once: school, work, marriage, motherhood. The weight of the world was on my shoulders, and I felt like I was barely surviving.

Like being a middle child, being in the middle of life is often overlooked. We tend to focus on either the beginning or the end. The beginning holds so much promise and potential, while the end often signifies a culmination of all your hard work and effort. But what about everything in between? What about those years when we're not quite children anymore but are far from the responsibilities of being adults? What about when we are in our thirties, forties, and fifties working hard to achieve our goals while also raising a family? During these unassuming stretches, life can be the most rewarding and revealing. In years without milestones, we can discover who we are underneath all our struggles, fears, doubts, and insecurities.

There will be times when we feel like we are on top of the world and times when we feel like we just can't go on anymore. There will be days where everything feels amazing and days where we just want to curl up in a ball and cry. Such is life's pendulum. We weave back and forth in these experiences. But the intervals between them are just as beautiful and full of surprises. Please embrace the in-between. The middle doesn't call attention to itself, but we need to appreciate it anyway.

We need to embrace and celebrate the all-nighters spent trying to catch up on studying, the dinners at BBQ restaurants because you forgot to defrost the chicken, and the home movies of your beautiful only-this-age-once daughters running around in their diapers. Because in the end, it is these moments that make up our lives.

Also, if you have a middle child or sibling, now would be a great time to go give them a hug.

CHAPTER 12

The Anatomy of Tenacity

Sometimes I think back to the three times I took classes on Anatomy and Physiology (don't judge! I had goals.).

I remember flipping through the textbooks where they showed the complexities of the body. There were diagrams of layer after layer of colorful organs, tissue, bone, and muscle that were intricate and in sync. The human form could be truly beautiful if it weren't so mysterious.

So much of what we are is visible on the outside, but how much more goes on that is unseen? Our system's design keeps us alive and thriving. Silent and humming behind the scenes. Even when trauma occurs, another body part can often compensate for the injured body part or work with us to push forward in a way we didn't think physically possible. Not to be outdone, our psyche and determination are also no strangers to this adaptation of surviving and thriving.

If we were able to sketch it out, what would the anatomy of tenacity look like? Would the outer layer look like a tough shell, or would it look like *zero fucks given* while tears fall from burning red eyes? Is it possible that what is next underneath would be crisscrossed layers of obstinance or optimism? What is the skeletal structure that keeps us together in one whole piece when it seems our world has turned against us?

Would the paradox of a heart be at the center or somewhere else? Tenacity's *thump thump thump* keeps beating even though it is both hard-shelled while also suffocating in the emotion that spills over. All sides of tenacity's paradox can burn while also filling us with a new perspective. Tenacity is the willingness to push past the hardships that want to slay us. Tenacity can be about picking ourselves up and trying again instead of giving up when all the obvious answers have been exhausted. Tenacity presents itself as drive, determination, and a deep stubbornness to break the mold and keep us alive in the often painful bullshit of life.

At the ripe old age of twenty years old, I met this new level of determination face to face. I thought I knew what it looked like. I'd had been through a lot by that point in my life, but I had not yet met *her*.

She was born tenacious and fiery from the start—Angelica Celeste, my little angel from heaven. A nurse from the hospital asked me, "What's her name?" as she admired her. I told her, and a slow grin moved across her kind face. "Ooh, Momma, you're gonna pay for that one," as if naming my baby after a heavenly host was a surefire ticket to Spicy Kiddo Town, USA. Well, she wasn't wrong.

My eldest daughter's vivacious personality was (and still is) a loud anthem of kick-adversity-in-the-balls. Becoming her mom changed my life and forever changed my perspective on what is possible if we decide it is.

When Angie was born, there was a cursory show-the-mom-the-baby pass, and then the doctors whisked her away.

But they didn't tell my husband or me anything. We were so young. We didn't know better. After about an hour, I pressed the red assistance button.

"Hi there, how can I help you?" a chipper nurse's voice rang through the staticky speaker.

"Um... yeah?" I said with my voice so tentative that the end turned up like a question. "Can I please have my baby back?"

Within ten minutes, the labor and delivery room filled with a horde of doctors—pediatricians, neonatologists, a pediatric pulmonologist, and more. I didn't know where to look. I felt overwhelmed. "What's going on? Where... where's my baby?"

One by one, the doctors of each specialty broke down their findings in words my husband and I could only sort of understand. One kind doctor stepped forward from the group and began to explain the situation as they knew it. He spoke to us in basic terms, probably because our mouths were open in dumbfounded shock and our worried, confused eyes showed our ignorance of all things medical emergency.

"Mr. and Mrs. Gonzalez, your baby is very sick. She's not breathing the way she needs to on her own, and we aren't sure why yet."

He went on to explain the baby had a blockage in her lung, which they *thought* might be a herniated diaphragm, but they weren't equipped at the hospital to diagnose her properly. Angie was breathing with support and was in critical condition. An ambulance was on its way to drive her the forty minutes to the Children's Hospital. I would have to stay behind.

I turned to my husband and tightly grabbed his forearm, "Honey, please go with her. She can't be alone. She needs us." I was scared to stay behind, but at least she would have her dad.

Angie did need her parents, but little did I know, my little angel was giving the nurses a run for their money behind the scenes.

Right before they wheeled her into my hospital room to say goodbye before being whisked away again, the doctor prepared me for what I was about to see. He told me Angie was in a medically induced coma for her own safety with the breathing tube.

"We tried to keep the medicine light, Mrs. Gonzalez, but she kept fighting and trying to yank the tube out. She almost succeeded, so we had to give her more medication to help her sleep deeper and keep her safe."

As terrified as I was, my heart floated with hope for my daughter. I clung to this crumb of evidence that my girl was already an eight-pound, four-ounce fighter.

Recently Angie said to me, "I describe myself as tenacious, and I would take it all the way back. I've been tenacious since I was born because I almost didn't make it. As a baby in the NICU, I decided I was gonna make it, and I was determined to survive."

So it was and so it is. That tiny, sick baby eventually became a cherub-cheeked, wide-eyed brunette toddler, frequently rocking pigtails that we called "spouty fountains" because of the way they erupted from her hair. She had eyelashes for days that framed the most beautiful brown eyes.

Angie was so strong that she was fire and ice. In a split second, she could flip between batting those lashes to get her way to narrowing her gaze in scathing disapproval at something we did. Tenacity in the toddler years looked like a lot of time-outs and screaming fits. She'd come out of time-out, more determined than ever to get her way. Nothing was going to stop this kid.

Growing up in school, Angie faced challenge after challenge. She didn't fit the mold behaviorally, so we got used to having parent-teacher conferences that opened with, "Well, Angie has a lot of friends, and she's really *social*," before they would launch into a speech that proved less that Angie wasn't a great student and more that the teachers weren't trying. We wouldn't know until later that this was because she had ADHD and other mental health concerns. Nonetheless, Angie pushed through the best she could and never let anyone mess with her, not even teachers.

"Determination? I feel like that's the one attribute of my personality that has never faded. No matter what, like if a teacher told me I can't do something, I was like, *Watch me*," Angelica recalled to me. She made the most of school by clinging to close friends, painting on large canvases at home after school, and although she didn't make the honor roll, she did her best and kept moving forward.

Years blurred by, and miraculously she finished high school. Just when she started post-high school, she was sidelined by a neck injury from a serious car accident. Despite the physical and mental trauma that ensued, she pressed forward.

She decided traditional college wasn't for her but wasn't sure what direction she was going to go. Angie always had a fascination with cutting and dying hair, so eventually, she decided to make it a career and go to cosmetology school. She got all set up, started attending classes, and even though she still had a hard time in school, Angelica knew she was doing the right thing. Slowly things were coming together... and then March 2020 happened.

"Even before the pandemic, going to school that often, or I was late a lot, or you know... there were a lot of times I just wanted to give up. I really wanted to drop out because I felt like I wasn't even worthy of this journey," Angie said.

Moving into the pandemic only compounded things. "Shortly before the lockdown, I lost my job. I got fired. So, for three months, I was just wasting away in my bed, making poor decisions."

Her cosmetology school scrambled to stay open with online classes, but it just didn't translate. With no job and no school, Angelica started to spiral—staying in her room almost twenty-four seven.

I wanted to let her find her own way, to make a change because she has always been one to decide on her own, or it won't happen. When I tried to convince her to find a job, she tried to convince me that she would try to sell her art instead.

It was a delicate balance of encouragement and gentle butt-kicking. As much as I wanted to take care of everything myself, as a mom who wanted the best for her, I needed her to find a reason for her to regain balance and a healthy routine.

The specifics of Angie's story may be different from yours, but what about you? Have you ever been tethered to your bed either literally or metaphorically, the world feeling like it's crumbling around you, and you don't know what to do? Maybe you do take after Ang and occasionally get up to feed yourself the bare minimum and then lay back down again. It's warm there. It's comfortable there. We know what to expect there. *Thump thump thump.* Tenacity is pounding from within, but can you hear it?

And then, seemingly out of nowhere, it was like Angie held a stethoscope to that resilient heart of hers and heard tenacity's call once again. She pulled herself up and abruptly started living again. She and her friend started talking about moving out on their own. *What?* This was a game-changer. Ang was twenty-one years old and had never been ready to even start discussing that before. This was no problem for her dad and me. We totally supported her. Here she was, wanting to take the next step into being an adult. There would be no outside pressure from us.

I asked her if she needed help finding an apartment. She already had one in mind and had a tour scheduled for the following Saturday. When I discovered she was going alone because her friend had to work, I slipped into mom mode and wanted to help. I held back at first because *What if this is something that she wants to do on her own?*

Tentatively, I asked, "Would you like me to go with you? I would love to see it with you, but it is totally okay if you don't want me to." The second part rushed out in one breath because the helicopter mom in me was hovering right under the surface, and I was not about to let that bitch out and ruin something.

"Mom, that would be awesome!"

She went on to show me that she had the application already filled out and ready to go. Unbeknownst to me, she had some savings, and her friend did as well, so they were set if this apartment was the right fit. And what do you know? It was the right fit!

Every detail I thought she might need help with or need info on, she had it covered. She set up her utilities, internet, and cable accounts by herself. She and her roommate figured out where to find a couch, side tables, dishes, and silverware. She managed all of this during a pandemic when even veterans of their industries didn't know their asses from their elbows.

I was blown away by Angie's rapid transformation. My little fighter had pulled herself up from the floor of the ring and was back in the center swinging again. This time she wasn't just winning the round. She wanted the whole damn match.

Right when Angie settled into her new cozy apartment and started working at a new job, her school opened back up. Just like that, everything fell into place. Angie started attending classes in person again, just with some safety precautions. This meant returning to taking on real clients. It meant transforming others from 'blah' to 'beauty' just as she transformed her own life in the span of a few months. Nothing in life was perfect, but Angelica's spirit came alive again, and she pressed forward even though this had been unfathomable less than a year prior.

Angie says her ultimate measure of success now is within. "It's continuing to take care of myself. I feel like that is successful. I am at my best when I can continue to do that without falling off."

She said that she knows that she will encounter tough stuff in the future, but the fact that she was once able to pull herself out of bed and into a new life with the sheer desire to live and do better for herself means it's possible. If she can do it once, she can do it again.

If we do this enough, we can find ourselves finishing school, getting a new job, maybe meeting that special someone, or traveling to a place we have never been before. Big things are totally possible but don't forget that they aren't the most important point. The real message is that we don't have to move mountains here. It is time to throw the covers back and sit up, put our feet on the ground, and *decide to stand*. It doesn't have to be a record-breaking leap. It could be a tiny, two-inch step you didn't take the day before.

Difficulties won't last forever. It might take a while to find the solution, no matter how small or obscure it might be, but know that everything will work itself out eventually.

You can choose to be a victim and complain about what you don't have. You can also choose to be the one that perseveres in the face of adversity. Success comes to the latter. This perseverance rarely comes with dogged independence. Fight. Fight for you even in the smallest of ways, and the snowball of change will come. Determination will build. Your spirit will return. Tenacity is a radical rebellion that revolts against the mediocrity that life tries to sneak in. It's a loud protest that says *I do not consent to this life. I'm better than this.* I'm not saying don't enjoy the little things. But we must push back on our self-imposed limitations. No more choking on the challenges and laying still when you need to move. If Angie can do it, we all can do it.

CHAPTER 13

All Hail the Shitty Rough Draft

Did you miss your Kindergarten calling to be a nurse, a firefighter, a doctor, or a lawyer?

Adults ask us from a very young age, "What do you want to be when you grow up?" because they expect us to magically know which aspirations will be relevant for the rest of our lives. The universal answer? "I have no idea." And hell, I still answer that way, and I'm a middle-aged business owner.

My daughter's early interest in hair worked out to be a career path, but that doesn't happen for most of us. Figuring out our life in advance is an impossible task to pose on ourselves. No one knows the direction of their life's path at any given time.

Eighteen-year-old high school seniors choose a college that aligns with what they think they want as a career later in life. College students repeatedly hear, "What's your major?" Their answer becomes a measure of which box to classify them in. God forbid those college students get going in their chosen program and decide to change majors! What if their insides are silently screaming, HOLY SHIT, I DO NOT WANT TO DO THIS FOR THE REST OF MY LIFE? Which box should we put them in then?

Some students feel pressure to finish out their academic careers and get started in the field. After all, it's the "right thing to do," and it will be what earns them all their monies. Despite all the internal pull away from their current path, they rationalize staying the course. *I can't change paths now, I'm up to my neck in student loans, and I will have wasted all that time.*

Reality check, my friends: you can course-correct at any time. It may feel like you can't, I know. But it is 100 percent possible, and if you stay in something you hate out of obligation, you will absolutely regret it. Just because the salary of your imposed career and aspirations feels "appropriate" for your schooling or experience, your soul can still die a little more every day that you clock in at work. Your worth has absolutely nothing to do with your bank account, your student loan balance, or how many hours you log at work to climb the corporate ladder. Main characters are important, and you are a living, breathing protagonist in your own story. In case no one has told you lately, you're sort of a big deal.

I used to beat myself up about job-hopping so much. I thought that longevity in a job determined my viability for my future professional advancement. Horseshit. I had to learn to reject the feeling that I was a bad employee or disloyal. My experience, knowledge, and interests bring value, not a date range on my LinkedIn profile. Even if I only stayed at a job for a short time or if it ended in termination, my resume is only a piece of paper flatly describing this multi-passionate, multi-faceted human being. Living these experiences, we filter out the qualities of who *we* will accept as our future collaborators or employers, not the other way around. We're the shit, remember? This is not just any journey. This is *our* journey.

Documenting my life story started with the roughest of drafts. I was learning to write my name when I was around five years old. Although I couldn't yet write my full name, Amariah, I decided to work on Riah. I drew my best flower and proudly signed my autograph at the bottom of the page. I carried the crayon-covered paper around with me for the next hour. After the kids' program finished, I found my dad talking to a small group of gentlemen outside the main building of our church. I skipped up to him and called out, "Look, Daddy! I wrote my name!"

He took the paper and slowly started to chuckle. I knew he wasn't making fun of me, but I was embarrassed that he was laughing at me in front of other people.

"Good job, honey," he said with a twinkle in his eye, "but you spelled it backward."

I took the paper back and looked at it. It looked good to me. There, in my beginner's handwriting, was the boldly printed spelling of H-A-I-R.

One of my first literary works demonstrated that I look at life from a different angle, even from the start. Others may see it as backward, but I see a work of art.

The child version of me on that day may never have guessed that she'd write an entire book. After all, she couldn't even spell her own name correctly. But Grown-Ass Me (and you, my dear reader) are holding what I never thought possible. By the time you have gotten this far in the book, the first and subsequent drafts have come and gone. The editing, preparation, and publishing processes on this snapshot of my life story are complete. So much progress, but I'm not done yet. (Sequel, anyone?)

To this day, sometimes I ask God, "Please show me where this is going, and I will be patient on the road there." Unfortunately, that's not the way that this soap opera of life goes. We seek this assurance everywhere because we can get confused and lost along the way. Further compounding the existential search is the *audacity* to not follow society's expected timeline of life's milestones! Family, friends, and media can pester and make you feel like you are coming up short. *What the fuck am I doing on this rotating rock in space?*

Maybe you *aren't* supposed to be married and have babies right now. Just because "everyone else" has done it, it doesn't mean you are supposed to. The fact that your current reality is different than theirs doesn't make you weird or unworthy of being loved in that way. Those milestones are part of *their* journey. It may or honestly may not work out for them. I experienced this by having a family *too young*—still breaking society's timeline standards. I also experienced backlash. It's not the achieving of the actual milestone that checks the box for them. It's falling in line with expectations when it is deemed acceptable. Fuck that shit. Who has time for that?

So yeah, Brenda has a bomb-ass job, and you're salty. You both have the same degree and while she's making bank, you hustle through life and shake the dust bunnies out of your wallet at the end of the pay period. All feelings are valid but promise me not to linger in your jealousy too long. Comparison slaughters your joy and clouds the view of the gorgeous path waiting for you.

Your worthiness doesn't rely on being famous, rich, or even stable in any form. Believe it or not (but seriously, believe it!), this current version of you counts as a human. You are the hero of your own story.

This book that you are reading? It's a prime example of this theory. I'm spilling the tea about how I have fumbled through life. I've taken the wrong turn or been led astray so many times. (Side note—if I'm spilling so much tea, can it be Boba Tea? 'Cuz that shit is delicious, and hopefully, I won't spill it all.)

I am the CEO of my own business. Yay! Are you jelly, thinking I am making seven or eight figures? Not even close. I took a massive pay cut to pursue opening my business. Was I scared? Hell-to-the-yes. Is it the right thing to do? Also, hell-to-the-yes! The quality of life that being a business owner affords is more important than making money for someone else *at this stage of my story*.

Even so, I give myself full permission to change my mind in a few years, a decade, or even tomorrow. Maybe I'll get my MBA, become the oldest circus clown ever, or perhaps I'll apply to a million corporate jobs, convincing them that the sum of my resume uniquely matches their random open position. Whatever decisions I make, I'm at the helm of this god damn ship, and I need to steer in the direction of who the fuck knows where, but I'll know when I get there.

Does it bother me not to know what my future holds? Yeah, every fucking day. I am in my forties. I should have some semblance of a plan, and if I think about it too much, it's a little embarrassing. A "real professional woman" would have a retirement plan, medical benefits outside of my partner's employment, more funds to donate to charities, and more time to volunteer. But I just don't. That's not part of my story right now.

This novella consists of waking up at the ass-crack of dawn, clacking away at the computer, then endless meetings, driving around from errand to errand, and often ending my workday at 10 p.m. Some days it's exhausting, but more often than not, I fucking love it.

I submit the following evidence of badassery in taking the scary leap to freedom: I give myself permission to take a nap at 11:45 a.m. if I want to. I can sit in my home office and sip the Americano I bought from the local coffee stand, knowing damn well I totally could have made coffee at home. Lastly, if I want to work at 6:00 a.m., take all the midday off, and pick up again at 4:00 p.m. I can totally do that. I'm trying so hard to let this journey play out the way it's supposed to and honor what helps me be my best.

To make this hero's path continue authentically, I must bravely put one unsure foot in front of the other, then follow the signs as they come. There is no life GPS. Move fast (safely) and work hard in one direction. Eventually, I'll hit a full stop, pivot, and keep moving. Don't be fooled by the naps I've got. I'm still "Riah-overworking" from the block.

You don't need to have it all figured out right now. It's okay. Have you peeked behind you recently? You can't possibly deny your progress. You may see it as incremental or insignificant, but it adds zest and interest to the story. Soon enough, you'll look back and say to someone, "Remember that time...?" Even if that memory recounts the difficulties of a dark place that you navigated through, you made it out alive, scars and all. What's a good hero's journey without conflict?

Stop trying to define where you are going and just live it here and now.

Be broke and creative. Be rich in abundance of whatever the fuck interests you. Go to the park and revel in nature's beauty. You can even do it the "Washington-State-Riah-way" and sit in the already warm car with the seat heaters on while enjoying the miracle of trees around you. Eat peanut butter and jelly sandwiches when you can't afford DoorDash. Pretend it's gourmet and set a fancy table setting for yourself. Splurge on those long-ass, bedazzled nails you've wanted because it makes you feel good. You might have to sacrifice somewhere else to prioritize those bad boys but fuck it. Your wallet might complain, but looking down at your hands, you can live it up in your bougie-ass world. It's our story, we get to live it however we want.

Can we kill the shame if you move back home with your parents because the outside world is impossible to afford? It's a temporary plot twist, not a failure. You identified a need and advocated for addressing that need. How can that be bad? Many of us silently suffer in unnecessary independence when help is available. Instead, you took care of yourself. The time for venturing back out will come before you know it (because who wants to live at home for that long? Middle-aged parents can be well-intentioned but annoying.). You've got this.

Live your job like it's a side hustle and your life like it's the main adventure. Find an amazing hobby that makes you giddy. My current obsession is making custom bookmarks out of epoxy resin. Think you don't have time or funds to start a hobby? Oftentimes you don't have to spend a lot of money. I found supplies in my local "Buy Nothing" group on Facebook (a community-based group that shares odds and ends with each other to save them from the landfill). I purchased used supplies on OfferUp, and I scoped out deals. I'll be damned if I live a life where I don't try new things and *have fun*. It's possible I will hate this hobby in a week, so maybe it is a "waste of time." But wouldn't it be worse if I didn't try and have fun at all because the hobby didn't fit into what I thought I was *supposed* to be doing?

Hear me on this: if you have it all figured out, *you are either lying or you are doing it wrong.* Every single one of us is mid-journey. If you limit yourself to one mapped-out path, you will miss all the juicy adventures you are destined for. Stick around, bestie. You are a page-turner and soon-to-be bestseller.

CHAPTER 14

Boom.

When was the last time you really looked at your reflection in the mirror? Not to check your hair, brush your teeth, or double-check the 'fit before you leave for the day. When was the last time you made meaningful eye contact with yourself?

I'll admit that although I have gorgeous green eyes (if I do say so myself), I rarely look at them. Sometimes I'm just evading the wrinkles now forming around them, but often I'm avoiding the deep thoughts that come with peering into your soul and giving yourself an internal gut check.

Your reflection can be a powerful tool.

In a dream I had a few years ago, I found myself standing and looking in a mirror. I spun around in a circle, and the mirror followed and surrounded me. Instead of my exact reflection, there were dozens of *me* from every age so far in my life. I saw myself as a baby with my little curly mop of red hair and fat cheeks. I saw myself as a grade-schooler in her homemade ripped jeans, and further down the line, I realized how truly beautiful I had been as a young woman. None of us spoke at first. We just looked at each other. Why were we here?

Timid at first, a half-pint version of me walked to the middle where I stood to show me an art project she had been working on. "That's so cool!" I told her, and I meant it. Her freckled face broke out into a crooked-toothed grin.

I moved my head around slowly to see if any other *me's* would also come forward.

"How come no one likes me?" Third grade me sobbed and tried to stop her tears as quickly as they came by rubbing her eyes. Her head hung low as she came to me.

"Hey, you can cry," I said. "Tears are good for you. We need a way to let all the sad stuff out."

I reassured her she would have the best of friends later, and that it was okay to feel sad when people rejected us. I told her she was worthy, beautiful, and kind. I told her boys are stinky and not to worry too much about Gabe Walker. She giggled at that and walked back to her place in the circle, face still wet but no longer crying.

On and on it went. Not every *me* stepped forward but most wanted to share something they were excited about. Some needed hope. Some needed a hug.

I woke up the next morning feeling a bit haunted. I turned to the mirror by my bed and looked deep into my green eyes. There had been so many versions of me, and yet these green eyes stayed the same. Each version of me was waiting for someone else to tell them they were okay. They simply needed permission to extend love and acknowledgment to themselves.

It dawned on me. I didn't need to achieve good grades to be worthy of anything. I already was. Having parents that stayed married wasn't going to heal our family. I could heal myself. Boyfriends who mistreated me—and even the husband who most definitely does *not* mistreat me—don't determine my beauty. I decide I'm a fucking bombshell and—boom—just like that, I am.

Mirrors are a little funny. They can obscure your view if they are stained and dirty and not taken proper care of. Something or someone can also shatter them into tiny pieces. You may not be able to see yourself as clearly in these situations, but it's not impossible. If a build-up of grime blurs your view, take some Windex to that sucker. If the broken shards are lying at your feet, ask a friend to buy you a new pane of glass. If you are feeling strong enough, buy the replacement yourself. Once you hang it up and restore your ability to look confidently at yourself, lift your chin and take in your beautiful reflection.

Your true measure of being enough, your utmost worthiness, and your badass success stems from *inside of you*. No one can give that to you, and no one can take it away from you.

I recently asked my youngest daughter, Gabi, who is twelve, "What is success to you?"

She answered, "It's, like, achieving happiness. So, it doesn't really have to be a huge celebration. If it makes you happy, I consider that success. That little spark of the moment because it feels really good. Then it might go away. But it's something I need to feel because it tells me I've achieved something, you know, kind of important to me."

That's it. The spark is what we chase. The feeling of *Hell yeah, I did that.*

I asked her more about her personal experience of working through the hard stuff, even after achieving some level of her version of success.

"I guess the way I deal with it is by telling myself I'm allowed to make mistakes because we're not robots. So, in order to accept who you are and in order to move on from past things that have happened, you just need to accept that maybe what you did wasn't, like, completely okay."

I wonder how much heartache we could save ourselves by chasing the spark more and accepting the mistakes as part of the process. What if the twelve-year-old versions of us held the power of self-acceptance before they weathered the land mines of adolescence and adulthood ahead?

Gabi isn't superhuman. She's just a well-adjusted preteen dealing with the same worries and insecurities we all had at her age. But she also has the magic of balancing the spark and radical self-forgiveness that many of us were missing at her age. She's unlocked what we all still need, regardless of our age.

Way back in the introduction, I said this book is for you. It still is, but I was speaking to a scared, confused, floundering version of you that now exists in the past. That version of you was 36,000 words ago.

Since then, have you found the answers to your questions? Have you found comfort or companionship within these pages? Are you able to hear tenacity *thump thump thump*ing inside you again? I sincerely hope so.

But even if you haven't, I know you have it in you to wake up tomorrow, throw back the covers, stand up, and stare rejection down despite the fear, despite the pain. I know I will. I'll probably cry, but I'm a teary, badass motherfucker who refuses to give up.

* * *

It's late. I'm still here in my home office, and the soft noises of a sleeping house accompany me as I write. My heart feels full, not just with love from and for my family, but with the joy, hope, and encouragement I am sending through these pages to you, dear reader.

I imagine it's nighttime where you are too. I imagine that the most successful version of you (whether they are in the past, present, or future) stands at the end of a dock in front of a large lake. A majestic skyline full of colorful buildings spans across the horizon in front of you. Their twinkling lights reflected in the water illuminate you.

Well, that, and the impressive sparkler you are holding. You write your name in the sky with its light and admire its tiny, beautiful, fiery particles.

Boom. Boom. Boom. The sky erupts into falling colors and shapes, and a huge grin breaks out on your face. It's not the 4th of July. These fireworks are for you and you alone. Because fuck the United States, this is *your* Independence Day. There's no grand finale because this party is just getting started. The spark is ablaze in your hand.

Because you *are* doing it, sweetness.

You are already successful as fuck.

Acknowledgments

When setting out on a long journey you've never embarked on before, you never know how much work it will take to reach your final destination. I've discovered along my journey writing *Successful as F*ck* that publishing a book takes a village, and I am so grateful for all the support. Fulfilling this dream would not have been possible without you.

Thank you, first and foremost, to my family for supporting me every step of the way. Your resounding faith in my ability keeps me going. For my supportive SAF community (including my amazing editor, Caitlyn Conville, who rocked my face off)—you rallied around me from the very beginning, and I am blown away. Wow, just... wow. I'm humbled by your belief in me and this book's message. For preordering SAF while it was being crafted into its final genius, I would like to extend a sincere thank you to the following people:

Ismael Gonzalez Guerrero, Jenn Schwope, Dee Fretwell, Tammy Wood, Jerusha Gray, Jessica Reed, Alicia Lozano, Emily Lujan, Janice Cornthwaite, Jim Billington, Jessica Patterson, Tamara Lewis, Kendra Williams, Diana Fulbright, Katie McLaughlin, Autumn Gray Eakin, Tonya Gow, Kathleen McDermott, Suzie Cordova, Tracey Warren, Chanta King,

Dr. Jennifer Tam, Nanea Hoffman, Corie Cook, Eric Koester, Tiffani Patlan, Gabriela Manciulea, Megan Winkler, Jackie Murphy, Brittany Button, Sandra Spady, Denise Morrison, Dr. Marlena Jbara, Karly Grant, Amy Woidtke, Hope Everheart, Kelsey Kidwell, Nicole Laino, Jen Stokes, Kat Liberty, Lisa M. Randolph, Parchelle Tashi, Rachel Stoll, Erin Keam, Nnenna Vasquez, Christina Dyer, Casleah Herwaldt, Tiffany Barry, Kayleigh Larin, Alison Crosthwait, Rashida Gaye, and Tarryn Reeves. Gabrielle Thil, Stephanie Hill-Manuel, Jessica Reed, Priyanka Raha, Monica Monfre, Nicole Lavine, Wesley Reece, Miriam Works, CarYnn and Marshall Holding-Howell, Linda Barutha